easy to grow! Vegetables

easy to grow!
Vegetables

METRO BOOKS
NEW YORK

This 2011 edition published by Metro Books,
by arrangement with Ilex Press.

Metro Books
122 Fifth Avenue
New York, NY 10011

ISBN: 978-1-4351-2667-1

Color reproduction by Dot Gradations Ltd, UK
Printed and bound in Malaysia

10 9 8 7 6 5 4 3 2 1

The following pictures are reproduced with kind permission of GAP picture library and Dave Bevan, Juliette Wade, Jonathan Buckley, Clive Nichols, Howard Rice, JS Sira, Marcus Harpur, Maxine Adcock, Elke Borkowski, Jerry Harpur, FhF Greenmedia, Fiona McLeod, Geoff Kidd, Keith Burdett, Rob Whitworth and Jo Whitworth:
P.10; P.11; P.16; P.19; P.30; P.33; P.40; P.42; P.52; P.56; P.78; P.82; P.83; P.96; P99; P.100; P.108; P.110; P.119; P.125; P.127(R).

Line illustration on page 29 drawn by Trina Dalziel.

Color photography by Lucinda Symons on the following pages:
P.20(L,R); P.21(L,R); P.22(L,R); P.23(L,R); P.24(L,R); P.25(L,R); P.26(L,R); P.27(L,R); P.36(R); P.37; P.38(L,R).

The Ilex Press would like to thank Ginkgo Gardens for the kind use of their center

Hardiness zones are geographic areas defined by the lowest temperatures they commonly get during winter. How hardy a plant is will determine whether it will survive the winters in these zones.

H gives the height measurement of the plant when fully grown; S refers to its maximum spread.

Vegetables that are grown from seed in spring and pulled up before winter aren't affected by the winter low temperatures that define the different hardiness zones; so these vegetables are marked N/A (Not Applicable).

Contents

Basics

Tools and materials

Before you get started on your vegetable garden, you are going to need a basic set of tools. Always buy the best you can afford. Saving money on tools is a false economy. Choose those made from stainless steel with solid wood handles. Never buy unseen – try them out for size and comfort first.

It will make a big difference to your workload if your tools are comfortable to use. Take good care of them, as well. Clean off mud and soil after use and wipe them over with a cloth before putting them away. Service them regularly and sharpen them as necessary and they will last you for years.

Basic set

Spade: An essential tool, needed for heavy digging, breaking up clods, moving soil. They come in many different sizes and shapes, which is why you need to try them to find the one that suits you best. Make sure that the tread on the shoulders fits your foot comfortably, as well.

Fork: Used for loosening soil and breaking it down, especially after digging, and for lifting plants. The prongs are either round or flat – though if you are only buying one, the latter may be more useful, as they do the minimum of damage to tubers when lifting potatoes and other roots.

Rake: Used for levelling soil, preparing seedbeds, removing stones and debris. Widths vary, but an 8 to 10-tooth rake is adequate for most purposes. It is very important to make sure the weight and balance are right for you, as it is difficult to work with one that is too heavy or cumbersome.

Hoe: You will need two types: the Dutch hoe, which has a flat rectangular blade that is used, as you walk backwards, to remove weeds, loosen soil or draw a drill; and the draw or swan-necked hoe, which has a blade at right angles to the handle. This is pulled towards you rather than pushed away, and is useful on heavier soils and for earthing up.

Hand trowel and fork: The trowel is a versatile tool, but is primarily used for planting. The fork is useful for weeding near plants and loosening soil. They need to be sturdy and well-made. They come in different shapes and sizes, so take your time to find the one that is most comfortable for you.

Garden line: Essential for making sure your rows are straight when planting seeds. You can buy them, or make your own by tying twine to two short canes.

Cultivator: Not essential, but the three to five claw-like prongs are useful for breaking up ground and weeding between plants.

Mattock: This is a heavy chisel-bladed hoe, again not essential, but sometimes easier to use on hard ground.

Pocket knife: Invaluable for slitting open bags of compost or manure, cutting twine, taking cuttings, etc.

Sharpening stone: Useful to have, to keep edges sharp and well maintained.

Secateurs/shears: For pruning, cutting, keeping things tidy.

Others

Watering can: Chose a sturdy one – plastic or metal – with a capacity of 1½–2 gallons (seven to nine liters). You will need two detachable roses – one coarse and one fine – so you can match flow to plant.

Wheelbarrow: For moving large amounts of soil, manure, plants, bags and so on. Again, size and balance is personal and you may find a second-hand one does the job as well.

Bucket: For holding soil and liquid materials, or moving quantities of stuff around the plot.

Carrying sheet or bag: Keep nearby while working

Hand tools
Good quality hand tools with solid wood handles will last longer and make gardening much easier.

to save time on trips to the compost heap or shed.
Bamboo canes: A selection of various sizes for marking out areas or positions, and providing support for plants, nets and wire.
Twine: For tying up branches, stems, canes, wires, etc.
Gloves: Choose a lighter, supple pair for pruning and planting, and a heavy duty pair for messier jobs such as handling prickly and stinging plants.
Frost protection fleece: To protect plants from the cold or pests, or to warm up the ground.
Cloches: A variety of different shapes, sizes and materials, including glass, plastic and polyurethane. For covering rows or individual plants – useful if you want to bring forward or extend the growing season, or for warming up the soil prior to sowing or planting.
Cold frames: Used for bringing on young plants or protecting a growing crop. They can be static with a solid floor, or movable (without a floor) to offer protection for plants growing in the ground, or adapted to make a hot bed.

For sowing seeds

Seed trays and small pots: Made of plastic (though wooden and terracotta types are also available) and used for sowing seeds that need to be pricked out when they have germinated.
Seed cells: For sowing individual seeds to grow on to the planting out stage.
Biodegradable pots: Used for sowing crops that do not like their roots disturbed. Once the seedling is large enough to be planted out in the ground, the whole thing can go in and the container will rot down as the plant grows.
Dibber: A pointed metal or wood tool used to make holes for planting seeds or young plants. A small one is used for pricking out seedlings.
Labels and markers: Essential so you know what is where. Many different types are available in plastic, wood or slate with an appropriate pencil or pen.
Propagator lids: Usually made of clear plastic and put over seed trays to speed up germination. You could also use cut-off plastic bottles set over individual pots.
Electric propagator: A small unit in which seeds are placed when a specific temperature is needed to germinate them (usually 55–61°F/13–16°C). The heat source may be a light bulb, heated plates or coils. Not essential, but a useful piece of equipment to have and they are usually inexpensive to run.

Deciding what to grow

Gardeners want to grow their own vegetables for a variety of reasons. You may, for example, wish to control what you eat, which means growing produce organically and avoiding the use of potentially harmful chemicals and fertilizers necessary for higher yields of commercial production. There is also the pleasure of eating garden-fresh produce.

Home-grown vegetables have a fullness of flavor that is lost in store-bought food. Another attractive aspect to growing them is the opportunity to experiment by producing more exotic and unusual fruit and vegetables that are either not available in most shops or are just too expensive to buy.

The ornamental potager

There is no reason why your vegetable garden should be any less attractive than the flower garden. A mixture of vegetables and herbs laid out in a square design, with perhaps an edging of clipped boxwood, will turn the edible garden into an object of beauty. You can make a very simple square design with just a few rows of vegetables or opt for a series of squares, with brick paths in between each square, to make a more elaborate potager. Herbs are ideally suited to this kind of design, and your potager could devote one or two squares to them. Site such a potager near the house, to make access easier. Additionally, soft fruit, such as gooseberries, can be trained as ornamental standards, and tree fruit can be fan-trained on wire supports, taking up minimal space and adding to the attraction of the garden.

Growing your own
Vegetables and herbs not only taste good but can also look good if they are well laid-out.

Planning an attractive vegetable plot
Growing edible crops can be as satisfying visually as it is in culinary terms, as this elegant vegetable plot demonstrates.

A year in the vegetable plot

EARLY SPRING

GENERAL TASKS

- Prepare seedbeds and cover with cloches or black plastic to warm up.
- Check beds are ready for the new season's crops and all weeds and roots have been removed.
- Feed over-wintered crops with a general fertilizer or mulch.
- Keep an eye on weeds and watch out for early signs of pests. Cover vulnerable plants with netting or fleece.
- Order seeds and young plants from mail-order companies.
- Check stored vegetables regularly and get rid of any that show signs of deterioration.
- This is the start of the busy season for sowing seeds, pricking out and potting on – check there is plenty of space in cold frames as well as the greenhouse and shed.

TIME TO SOW

In situ: American land cress, beet, fava bean, carrot, belgian endive (heading), kohlrabi, pea (earlies), radish, rocket, spinach, scallion, turnip.

In a nursery bed: Brussels sprout (earlies), cabbage (fall and winter), globe artichoke, leek, lettuce.

Under glass: Eggplant, broccoli (calabrese), cauliflower (summer), chard, celery, okra, onion, pepper, pumpkin, shallot, squash, indoor tomato.

TIME TO PLANT/TRANSPLANT

In situ: Asparagus, cabbage (summer), cauliflower (summer), garlic, globe artichoke, Jerusalem artichoke, onion, potato (earlies), shallot.

Under glass: Early salad leaves, tomato.

IN SEASON

American land cress, Brussels sprout, broccoli (sprouting), cabbage, cauliflower, celeriac, celery (trench), chard, belgian endive (forced), corn salad, leek, lettuce, parsnip, pumpkin, radish, rhubarb (forced), spinach, scallion, rutabaga, turnip top.

LATE SPRING

GENERAL TASKS

- Begin to move young plants outside to start the hardening-off process.
- Keep an eye on the soil and water if it becomes very dry. Mulch when the soil is moist to help retain water.
- Hoe regularly to keep on top of weeds and check for signs of pests and disease – especially under cloches or fleece.
- Stay on top of thinning out, earthing up potatoes and providing support for climbers such as peas and beans.
- Clear beds of overwintered vegetables. Store remaining crops and add stumps, roots and any that are not good enough to keep to the compost heap.
- Prepare beds for new crops: put in supports for netting or wire cages; erect cane supports as required; dig a trench for celery and prepare planting holes for cucurbits.

TIME TO SOW

In situ: American land cress, asparagus, beet, fava beans, broccoli (calabrese), carrot, chard, belgian endive (heading and forcing), endive, fennel, kale, kohlrabi, lettuce, onion (bulbing and scallion), parsnip, pea, spinach, radish, rocket, rutabaga, turnip.

In a nursery bed: Brussels sprout, cabbage (fall and winter), cauliflower (fall and winter), kale, leek, broccoli (sprouting).

Under glass: Beans (borlotti, green and scarlet runner), cardoon, zucchini, cucumber, pumpkin, squash, corn, tomato (outdoor).

TIME TO PLANT/TRANSPLANT

In situ: Asparagus, cabbage (summer), globe artichoke, Jerusalem artichoke, early brassicas, onion, potato.

Once all danger of frosts has passed: Eggplant, celeriac, celery, beans (borlotti, green and scarlet runner), pea (earlies), pepper, corn, tomato (outdoor).

Under glass: Eggplant, cucumber, tomato.

IN SEASON

American land cress, asparagus, fava bean, broccoli (sprouting), Brussels sprout, cabbage, carrot, cauliflower, chard, kale, leek, lettuce, radish, rhubarb, scallion, spinach, turnip, turnip top.

EARLY SUMMER

GENERAL TASKS

- Sow intercrops such as lettuces where there is space. Lightly fork over the ground and add fertilizer first.
- Apply a general fertilizer or high-potash feed to plants that need it, such as squashes, cucumbers and tomatoes.
- Watch for pests and take precautions. Keep on top of watering and weeding.
- Stake, tie in and train sideshoots on crops like beans, cucumbers and tomatoes.
- Order in any seedlings or young plants needed for fall and winter sowings.
- Start harvesting crops as they are ready.
- It's easy to forget at this time of year to continue with successive sowing to provide a continuous supply of crops. Sow seeds in situ, or under cover for transplanting later.

TIME TO SOW

In situ: American land cress, beet, cardoon, carrot, chard, belgian endive (forcing and heading), zucchini, chicory (frisée), fennel, kale, kohlrabi, lettuce, pea, radish, scallion, spinach, squash, rutabaga, corn, turnip.

In a nursery bed: Winter brassicas.

TIME TO PLANT/TRANSPLANT

In situ: Beans (borlotti, green and scarlet runner), brassicas (fall and winter), celery, cucumber, globe artichoke, leek, lettuce, okra, pepper, pumpkin, squash, corn, tomato.

IN SEASON

Asparagus, fava bean, broccoli (calabrese), cabbage, carrot, cauliflower, chard, corn salad, endive, kohlrabi, American land cress, lettuce, onions (scallion and over-wintered bulbs), pea, potato, radish, rhubarb, spinach, turnip.

LATE SUMMER

GENERAL TASKS

- Keep picking repeat-producing crops such as beans, zucchini and tomatoes to encourage more to grow.
- Clear away crops that have finished and dig over the ground to expose any pests or weeds in the soil.
- Pests and diseases spread quickly in hot, dry weather, so stay vigilant. If it's wet and humid, watch for potato blight, which thrives in those conditions.
- If you have suitable space, plant up a green manure crop.
- Clear cold frames and the greenhouse ready for sowing and growing winter crops that need protection from frosts.
- Weed, mulch and water.

TIME TO SOW

In situ: American land cress, beet, carrot, chard, belgian endive (heading), Chinese cabbage, corn salad, endive (broad-leaved), fennel, kohlrabi, lettuce, mizuna greens, onion (bulbing and scallion), bok choy, pea (fall), radish (summer and winter), spinach (winter), turnip.

In a nursery bed: Cabbage (spring and red varieties), kale.

TIME TO PLANT/TRANSPLANT

In situ: Broccoli (sprouting), cabbage (spring), cauliflowers (fall and winter), kale, leek.

IN SEASON

American land cress, eggplant, beet, borlotti bean, fava bean, broccoli (calabrese), cabbage, carrot, cauliflower, celery, chard, corn salad, cucumber, endive, green bean, garlic, globe artichoke, kohlrabi, leek, lettuce, onion (bulbing), potato, radish, scarlet runner, salad onion, shallot, spinach, squash, corn, tomato, turnip.

EARLY FALL

GENERAL TASKS

- Cover late and overwintering crops with cloches or fleeces if the weather turns cold.
- Clear spent crops and supports from beds ready for fall digging and liming.
- Cover root vegetables that are being left in the ground with straw, or lift and store in a frost-free place.
- Start gathering together used pots, seed trays, labels, canes, etc. and clean and store ready for future use.

TIME TO SOW

In situ: Fava bean, carrot, pea, rocket, spinach (winter).

In a nursery bed: Cabbage (spring), cauliflower (summer).

Under glass: Lettuce, mizuna greens, bok choy, radish.

TIME TO PLANT/TRANSPLANT

In situ: Cabbage (spring), garlic, onion (fall).

Under glass: Lettuce.

IN SEASON

Eggplant, beet, broccoli (calabrese and sprouting), Brussels sprout, cabbage, cardoon, carrot, cauliflower, celeriac, celery, belgian endive (heading), cucumber, endive, fennel, green bean, Jerusalem artichoke, kale, kohlrabi, leek, lettuce, mizuna greens, okra, onion, bok choy, parsnip, pea, pepper, potato, pumpkin, radish, scarlet runner, spinach, squash, rutabaga, corn, tomato, turnip.

LATE FALL

GENERAL TASKS

- Clear all non-hardy crops and dig over the ground. If it's heavy, leave clods on top to allow the frost to break it down.
- Lift and store any remaining winter crops that are at risk of severe weather. Check any stored crops are still in good condition.
- Earth up stems of cabbages, cauliflowers and Brussels sprouts to protect from wind rock.
- Gather leaves together to make your own nutritious leaf mold to use as a mulch (it should be ready in a year). Erect a simple structure of wire netting wrapped around three or four stakes and pile in the leaves, pushing down firmly. Or pack them into black

plastic bags, punch in a few holes and leave to rot – this may take longer than a year.

TIME TO SOW

In situ: Fava bean, carrot, pea.

Under glass: Lettuce, mizuna greens, bok choy, radish, rocket.

TIME TO PLANT/TRANSPLANT

In situ: Cabbage (spring), garlic, onion (fall).

IN SEASON

American land cress, Brussels sprout, cabbage, carrot, cauliflower, celeriac, celery, chard, belgian endive (heading and forced), Chinese cabbage, corn salad, endive, fennel, kohlrabi, Jerusalem artichoke, kale, leek, lettuce, mizuna greens, okra, bok choy, parsnip, potato, pumpkin, radish, rhubarb, spinach, rutabaga, turnip.

WINTER

GENERAL TASKS

- Carry on with digging and preparing soil as weather permits.
- Continue to check stored crops regularly for signs of mold, pests or diseases.
- Clean cloches and cold frames that are not in use.
- If bad weather is forecast, lift a supply of fresh vegetables so you do not need to do so in the snow or frost.
- Check compost bins: empty them out, mix the contents together, then refill.
- Put out cloches, cold frames, black plastic or straw to warm up beds ready for early plantings.
- Clean and sharpen tools for the start of the new gardening year. Check over equipment – including sundry items such as seed trays, canes, labels, string, etc. – replacing or supplementing where needed.
- On a fine day, walk round your plot to remind yourself of the year's successes and failures, making notes if necessary, to help plan next year's crops and rotations. Order in seeds and young plants.

TIME TO SOW

Under glass: Eggplant, beet, fava bean, cabbage (summer), carrot, cauliflower (summer), celeriac, celery, cucumber, leek, lettuce, onion, radish, salad onion, spinach.

TIME TO PLANT/TRANSPLANT

In situ: Garlic, globe artichoke, rhubarb, shallot.

IN SEASON

American land cress, broccoli (sprouting), Brussels sprout, cabbage, carrot, cauliflower, celeriac, celery, belgian endive (forced and heading), corn salad, endive, fennel, Jerusalem artichoke, kale, kohlrabi, leek, lettuce, mizuna greens, bok choy, parsnip, radish, rhubarb (forced), spinach, rutabaga.

Choosing and buying plants

How long crops take to grow, whether continuity is required, how much time is available and the skill of the gardener are all major considerations when planning a vegetable garden, since these will influence the time needed to tend the plot. Inexperienced gardeners should try not to be too ambitious at first and thus risk disappointment; they should start with fast-maturing salad crops.

As gardeners become more experienced and skilled, they can gradually experiment with vegetables that are more difficult to grow. One advantage of short-term crops is that they often allow several cropping cycles in each year, which is a quick way to gain tangible results – and if something does go wrong, the mistakes will have no long-term implications.

Buying plants

Make a list of all the plants that you want to grow and stick to it. Remember that plants get bigger; don't worry if the beds look a bit bare when first planted, as they will soon fill out.

Fast-growing crops
Quick-maturing carrots and beets allow you to re-use the space within one growing year.

The most important thing to consider when growing any vegetable is the direction of the sun. In the northern hemisphere, if a garden or vegetable plot faces south, is sheltered, and the general climate is hot enough, heat-loving vegetables can be grown. If the vegetable plot faces north, then you should concentrate on those plants that will flourish in a degree of shade.

It is important to plan purchasing and planting carefully. Make a list of the vegetables that you plan to grow then check whether there is a specialist nursery near you. If there is you can purchase the plants you require in person, but you may have to order them to be sent by mail. Nurseries are used to sending plants through the mail, and it is seldom that plants arrive in anything other than good condition.

It is best to buy plants and seeds from a specialist nursery rather than from a general garden center or supermarket where the choice may be limited and, usually, no specialist advice or help is available.

Bare-root plants

Plants should be planted at the right time of the year and this applies particularly to vegetables. Generally these are always best planted in the fall when the growth is dying down but there remains enough warmth and moisture in the soil to let the root system establish itself. Also, for fruit trees you are better to purchase bare-root plants than trees and shrubs that have been container-grown, as these will generally be healthier and in better condition overall.

Plants grown in open soil and lifted as "bare-root"

plants often do much better than those raised and bought in plastic containers. Plants raised in containers often have restricted root systems which never fully recover even when planted out. Bare-root plants are only available when they are dormant, in the winter time, so this does restrict when you can plant them.

Heeling in

If you cannot plant large vegetables as soon as they arrive, dig a small trench in a container, lay the plants in it at an angle of 45 degrees and cover them firmly with soil until you have time to complete the planting properly. The vegetables are unlikely to come to too much harm if they are not left for too long. If a frost threatens, protect the plants by covering them with garden fleece or some sacking.

Buying plants in person

If you plan to buy young vegetable plants yourself at a garden center, rather than growing them from seed, there are a number of things to look out for. Check all the leaves for signs of pests or disease (see pages 44–45), and make sure that the plant does not suffer from leaf drop. Avoid plants that have moss growing on the top of the container, as this indicates that they have been there for too long. Check to see that there are not too many roots growing out of the holes at the foot of the container for the same reason.

Plug plants (young vegetable plants, usually sold in packs of six) are a great, easy way to grow vegetables and especially helpful if you're just starting out or don't have much time. The choice will be more limited but the more tricky jobs of sowing seeds and pricking out are done for you.

Slow-growing crops
Slower-maturing maincrop potatoes and onions occupy a section of the plot for most of the year.

Designing your plot

Many people grow vegetables only if they can find some spare room in the garden, while for others the challenge is to produce a year-round supply of home-grown food. The planning and layout of a vegetable plot and types of vegetable chosen will be influenced by the number of people who want to eat home-grown vegetables and the vegetables they like the most.

It should be possible to keep a family of three supplied with vegetables year-round from a plot measuring around 21 x 12ft (7 x 4m), but a good supply of produce can actually be grown on an area much smaller than this. Where space is limited, greater yields can be produced by plants that grow vertically rather than those that spread sideways.

Choosing a suitable site

The ideal site in which to grow vegetables is one that is warm and sunny during the growing season, and has plenty of light and good air circulation, while being sheltered from strong winds (since wind exposure can reduce plant growth by up to 30 percent). The air flow is particularly important for wind-pollinated crops, such as corn, and to reduce the incidence of pests and diseases, which is worse in still air conditions.

A gently sloping, sunny site is perfect for an early start in spring, because it will warm up slightly quicker than other aspects. On steeper slopes, plant across the slope rather than down it, because this will reduce soil erosion during heavy rain.

Planning the vegetable plot

An efficient vegetable garden should be planned to make the best use of sun, shelter and space. The vegetables should be planted in rotation groups (see pages 28–29) to ensure pests do not build up.

It is important that you organize your vegetable plot as efficiently as possible, to ensure that the crops are rotated correctly and that you make the maximum use of the available sun and shelter.

Plant the tallest crops (such as Jerusalem artichoke or scarlet runner) so that they do not block the light from the smaller-growing vegetables. Use the walls or fences for shelter, and for supports for beans, peas or cordon or espalier fruit trees.

Remember to leave yourself ample space to walk between the blocks or rows of vegetables. Trampling on the soil will destroy its structure and reduce its potential yield.

Growing in containers

Vegetables, fruit and herbs can all be grown in containers in the most unlikely of places – on patios, balconies, fire escapes and walkways, or on any small plot of ground where the light is good. You can even grow some vegetables on your windowsill!

Although you will naturally want to choose the most attractive container for your vegetables, for successful results the container's appearance is not nearly as important as the contents. Whatever the plant to go in the container, you need to fill it with fresh, well-balanced potting mix and a base dressing of fertilizer, adding further top-dressings of fertilizer throughout the growing season. Long-rooted vegetables such as carrots and parsnips require deep containers (at least 18in/45cm deep) in order to grow satisfactorily.

Tall crops tend to become unstable, especially if grown in small pots, and can blow over in strong winds, so protect these with stones or netting. Container-grown crops need to be watered frequently during warm or dry weather.

Organic gardening

You can help to achieve harmony in your garden by working with nature to replenish its resources as you make use of them. You can do this by feeding the soil with plant waste such as decaying grass cuttings or fall leaves that provide beneficial micro-organisms.

This is what organic gardening is all about – growing vegetables, herbs, flowers or ornamental plants using plant matter, compost and beneficial insects rather than synthetic products such as pesticides and fertilizers.

Compost bins are an essential part of organic vegetable gardening. Raw kitchen scraps as well as leaves and cuttings from the garden can all go into the bins.

Growing vegetables from seed

Seed is the means by which most vegetables reproduce themselves. Among all the methods of propagation that can be used with vegetables, growing from seed is the most common. It is much less expensive than buying already established plants, although the disadvantage is the amount of time involved in preparing and planting the seeds and then waiting for them to grow.

Many different kinds of vegetable are normally grown from seed. Vegetable seeds can vary enormously in size and can either be sown directly into the ground or sown in pots or seed trays and transplanted later. Seed packets will advise you on which method is most suitable for the vegetable of your choice. It can depend on how you will use the vegetable and the quantity you would like. Growing from seed is generally straightforward, but it is important to understand a little of their requirements.

DIRECT SOWING

Many vegetables can be sown directly into the ground where they are to grow. However, to achieve success and to have as many seeds germinate as possible, you must first ensure that the timing and conditions are just right. So the temperature must be suitable – most vegetables simply will not grow

1 Prepare a seedbed by clearing any existing weeds, making a reasonably fine bed without too many soil lumps or stones.

2 Mark out different areas for the vegetables to be planted using sand. Vegetables don't have to be grown in rows; a prettier arrangement might be more suitable for a garden setting.

Seed requirements

Seeds have certain basic requirements in order to germinate and grow.

- Moisture is supplied by moist compost or soil. Larger seeds can be soaked overnite to speed up their germination time.
- Oxygen is available in a well-aerated seed or potting compost, or in soil that is well cultivated. Waterlogged or compacted soil can cause failure.
- Warmth is required in varying degrees for successful germination. The optimum temperature is 68°F (20°C).
- Some seeds, particularly those of wild plants, require light to germinate. As a general rule, most small seeds should be surface sown or only lightly covered. Bury larger seeds to their own depth.

Germination time

On average, germination takes up to 30 days, but some seeds may take 90 days or more. If your seeds do not come up in reasonable time, take a look at them to find out what has gone wrong. In some cases the seed may have rotted or gone soggy, in which case start again. If the seed is hard, it is still alive and is in dormancy, awaiting the right conditions to germinate. Seeds do this in order to give themselves the best chance of survival; without such safety mechanisms they might germinate during drought or when temperatures are too high or too low for survival. To improve their chance of survival, wild seeds do not always germinate all at the same time. This may give rise to erratic germination over a long period.

unless the average temperature during the day is above 43°F (6°C) – the soil must be well prepared and you must follow the seed company's guidelines as to planting depth and distance. In order for the seeds to germinate the earth must be warm enough and neither too dry nor too wet.

3 Sprinkle seeds over the soil. Dustlike seeds should be scattered on the surface. Larger seeds should be pressed into the soil, to the same depth as the seed size. Sow sparsely to avoid having to thin out the seedlings.

4 If the seeds need to be covered (see step 3), use your fingers or a small fork to work them lightly into the soil. Firm the soil down lightly and water with a fine rose.

Cold treatment or stratification

Some seeds will not germinate until they have been through the low and freezing temperatures of winter. In this way, nature ensures that they germinate in spring, when weather conditions are most favorable for growth. Sow these seeds in the fall, cover the tray with glass to protect against mice and birds, and leave it outside or in a cold frame over the winter. Germination will take place in early or late spring.

Alternatively, mix the seed with moist peat or sand in a plastic bag and leave outside over the winter (or in the refrigerator for approximately eight weeks). In the spring, sow as normal.

The seeds of some vegetables are contained in a fleshy coating. To germinate, the seed coat has to be broken down. In nature this happens when the seed passes through a bird's intestine. If you want to grow such seeds yourself, they should be stratified over winter, although some may take as long as two seasons to germinate.

Scarification

Seeds with very hard coats take a long time to germinate unless you break down the seed coat so the seed can absorb moisture. This treatment is called scarification. The easiest method is to soak the seeds in warm water for 24 hours.

Where the seed coat is very hard, you may have to wear it down in one of two ways:

Scraping Place small seeds in a jar lined with sandpaper and shake the jar.

Chipping Using a sharp knife, make a nick in the outer coat of large seeds.

Do not damage the inner, soft material, the part of the seed that will germinate, or the seed may rot.

INDOOR SOWING

Because some vegetables have tiny seeds and germination can take many weeks, even months in some cases, it is not always practical to sow in situ. Vermin or birds may take the seed; more usually, weed growth overtakes the sowing area, and distinguishing between weed and vegetable seedlings

1 Prepare the seed tray with special seed and sowing compost, level it off ¼in (0.6 cm) below the rim. Water with a fine rose until moist throughout.

2 Pour the seeds into the palm of your hand, pick some up between your thumb and forefinger, and sprinkle thinly and evenly over the surface of the seed tray. Do not sow too thickly.

Caring for seedlings

After direct sowing, always mark the area with sticks or stones or by sprinkling clean sand over the seeded area and label with the date and plant name.

If the season is windy, hot, or cold, you should cover the area with "fleece" to protect the seeds and prevent the soil from drying out. A featherlight, translucent fleece creates a warm microclimate and allows rain through; it also keeps off birds and pests.

Seed sown indoors

Seed trays should be kept in the shade, never in direct sun. Keep them in a warm place in the house or in a greenhouse.

When the seeds start to germinate, remove the glass cover. Do not overwater the seedlings or allow the seed compost to dry out. Keep them out of direct sun; high temperatures encourage spindly growth.

Because the seedlings have been growing in a protected environment, they need to be gradually acclimatized to conditions out of doors. This process is known as "hardening off." For a period of two to three weeks move the seedlings from the greenhouse to a closed frame or open the frame during the day, putting them back in the protected environment at nite.

Transplant the seedlings into small pots when they are large enough to handle. Allow them to become well rooted before planting.

Self-seeding

Some vegetables will self-seed if the flower heads are left for the seed to mature. In any natural or ecological planting this is desirable. Unwanted seedlings can be transplanted or hoed out.

can be difficult. It is often best to germinate small seeds in controlled conditions indoors, in a seed tray rather than in the open ground.

3 Lightly cover with fine seed compost sieved through a plastic pot or sieve. Cover larger seeds to their own thickness or press them into the seed compost. Tiny seeds germinate best uncovered. Water gently with a fine rose.

4 Cover the seed tray with a sheet of glass or a plastic lid. This keeps moisture in, helps to eliminate the need for further watering, and prevents pests attacking the seeds and emerging seedlings. Keep in the shade.

Preparing the site

Just as plowing is the farmer's way of moving the soil deeply in preparation for shallower cultivations and seed-sowing, digging is the basic cultivation of the gardener. You must dig any ground that is being cultivated for the first time or that has just been cleared of an old crop. A spade is the normal tool used for digging, but on heavy ground, a strong fork is much easier to use and just as effective.

The ideal soil for growing vegetables is a loam (a mixture of clay, sand, and silt in more or less equal proportions) containing humus (decaying organic matter) and with a pH, or acidity level, preferably between 6.5 and 7.0. Soils that vary from this ideal – that is, they are more sandy, or have little humus – may need more cultivation. Soil also needs to be fertile, which usually means adding fertilizers or well-rotted manure before sowing or planting (see pages 38–39).

There are several reasons for digging. The main one is to break up the soil so that excess water can drain away and roots can penetrate in their search for water and nutrients. As the ground is broken up, air is able to reach down into it so that the roots can

DIGGING THE SOIL

The depth of your topsoil, the quality of drainage in your garden and whether or not your plot has been previously cultivated, will all determine the best digging method to use. Single and double digging are the most effective and labor-efficient digging techniques for areas of ground. For single

1 When single digging a plot of land, use a line to mark out the position of the first trench. The trench should be 9–10in (23–25cm) wide.

2 Dig out the soil to a full spade's depth and use a wheel-barrow to move it to the far end of the plot, where it will be used to fill in the final trench.

"breathe." Digging also creates a suitable tilth for sowing or planting and is the most thorough and reliable way of burying bulky organic matter, such as garden compost, that is vital if the soil is to "live" and support good crops.

Basic cultivation

In order to grow worthwhile crops, you need at least a basic knowledge of soil cultivation and the tools required to carry it out. As well as a spade and fork, you will need a good, sturdy rake to break down the soil surface still further before sowing seeds. When sowing seeds or planting out seedlings, always use a garden line; never rely on drawing out a straight line by eye, as it will nearly always end up not being straight at all if you use this method.

Once the plants are growing, they will inevitably be challenged by weeds. The easiest way of dealing with these is to hoe them out, using either a Dutch or a draw hoe. Never try to cultivate the ground when it is wet enough to stick to the tools and always clean your tools after use. All garden tools can be made of either ordinary or stainless steel. Stainless steel costs more, but does not go rusty. As a general rule, always buy the best tools you can afford; the better they are, the longer they will last. If you maintain them properly as well, so much the better.

If the soil conditions are not suitable for the plants you want to grow, your results will be poor. Within the soil the most important material is the organic matter or humus. In nature this comes from decomposed vegetation, but in the garden you must add it in the form of garden compost or farmyard manure. Normal levels of organic matter contain only small amounts of the essential plant foods, so you will need to add these in the form of fertilizers. Under average garden conditions, add both bulky organic matter and plant foods to the soil at least once a year for it to remain in a suitable state for plants to grow well.

digging, follow the sequence shown here. Before commencing any digging, make sure that the site to be dug is clear of all persistent weeds, in order to reduce the competition that young plants face in their first weeks in the soil, when they need to bed in and establish themselves properly.

3 Turn around, so you have your back to the plot to be dug, and start on the next trench, turning this soil into the first trench.

4 Always keep the trench open and clear so that there is enough room to accommodate the next "row" of soil excavated from the previous trench.

Fertilizing the soil

For optimum results, soil that is intensively cultivated needs generous fertilizing. This can be provided with organic or inorganic matter. A great advantage of organic manures and fertilizers is that they encourage worm activity, which in turn aids soil fertility. Soil that has had no organic matter added is likely to have a worm count of 100–300 per sq yd (sq m) in the top 12in (30cm) of soil. This figure often increases to around 400–500 per sq yd (sq m) if organic matter is regularly added.

Although quite adequate crops of vegetables can be grown in soils where only organic manure and fertilizers are used, higher yields are usually achieved where inorganic, "chemical" fertilizers are incorporated. The amount of fertilizer needed will depend on the soil type, because light, sandy soils lose fertilizer quickly, whereas clay soils will hold nutrients for much longer. It is also affected by the kind of crop being grown: leafy crops, such as cabbages, need plenty of nitrogen, with one-third of this being provided when they are planted and the remaining two-thirds supplied while the plants are growing.

Vegetable crops growing through winter should get most of their nitrogen in spring rather than fall, because nitrogen encourages soft growth, and if large quantities of nitrogen are added in fall this could lead to the soft growth being killed by frost. Therefore, overwintering crops should be given a balanced fertilizer to toughen the leaves and stems. Fruiting crops such as tomatoes and peppers need regular fertilizing with phosphate and potassium fertilizers as soon as the plants start to flower in order to encourage good flower and fruit development.

Preparing the soil

The aim of tasks such as digging and raking the soil is to get the soil into the best condition possible for growing vegetables. Digging is the most important of these operations, because it allows air into the soil. This encourages the biological activity so essential for soil fertility, as well as raising clods of earth so that they can be broken up by frost.

IMPROVING SOIL

While we cannot completely change the basic soil type we have in the garden and must learn to live with it to a degree, we can temporarily alter its pH (by adding lime), feed it and improve its structure. The aim is to end up with soil rich in humus with a top layer of fine, crumbly tilth. Even if your soil is

1 Organic compost made from organic garden waste is an invaluable source of nutrients. Check that the compost is well rotted before you put it on the ground, as fresh compost will burn any plants it comes into contact with.

2 Spread a thick layer of well-rotted organic matter onto the soil surface. Use a spade or fork to remove the compost from the wheelbarrow and then rake it evenly all over the area to be cultivated.

No-dig method

Growing methods involving little or no cultivation are very popular, especially on light soils where the soil structure is easily damaged or where natural fertility is low. The no-dig, or "zero-cultivation," technique uses the resident worm population to cultivate the soil; layers of well-rotted organic matter are spread over the soil as a mulch and the worms incorporate this into the soil. Thus no digging is needed. Crop plants are inserted through the mulch, and when they have matured, the stalks are cut off at soil level and the new crop is planted between the rows of the previous crops, while the roots rot in situ.

Deep-dig method

The deep-digging method of soil preparation involves incorporating large amounts of compost or manure while double-digging a plot. This creates a deep, fertile rooting zone for the plants. Further dressings of organic matter are added at regular intervals, but there is no need for additional digging.

Difficult soils

The no-dig and deep-dig methods are ideal if you have a heavy soil that suffers from compaction when cultivated in wet conditions (although this problem may be overcome by working on wooden boards laid on the soil) or a light, sandy soil needing humus and fertility. These soils benefit from the lack of cultivation and the large amount of organic matter that is added.

Crops such as onions and lettuce, which can be planted close together, will usually do particularly well when they are cultivated in these kinds of soil.

Preparing a seedbed

Digging alone would leave the soil too uneven for growing most vegetables, so further cultivation is needed to produce a fine crumb structure, or "tilth," on the soil surface. This usually involves raking the soil several times to break down any lumps, and removing any stones you find, to create a fairly level, even surface.

naturally neutral and fertile, it will need a certain amount of organic material in order to remain so. While plants may grow happily in this type of soil in the first year, they will suck the nutrients out of it. The soil must be constantly replenished if you want to carry on getting a good harvest.

3 Dig the bed thoroughly with a garden fork, incorporating the compost and working it into the soil beneath the surface. The final bed should have a slightly domed surface, ready to receive the plants.

4 The bed is now ready for planting. Carefully remove the plants from their pots. Use a hand trowel to dig a hole to the depth of the rootball and place the plant in it. Backfill the hole and gently firm soil around the base of the plant.

Planting techniques

Vegetables tend to be relatively short-term crops, because most grow rapidly and are harvested before they reach maturity. There are various ways in which you can maximize the efficiency of your vegetable plot in order to achieve the best possible yield of a number of different crops at all times.

Planning to avoid a glut

Take care when planning your garden not to grow too many of one type of vegetable that will ripen all at the same time. Do not overestimate your requirements.

Try to time your planting to produce a staggered harvest. For example, in the summer you may only wish to eat a lettuce every other day – that is, seven in two weeks; don't therefore plant a dozen F1 hybrids that will mature at the same time, instead plant six and another six two weeks later.

Some crops, particularly the short-term salad crops, are the most susceptible to gluts and gaps, but this can be avoided to a large extent by sowing batches of seed on a planned basis. Timing of sowings can be difficult to gauge, but a good guide is to choose the date when you hope to harvest the crop and count back from there the number of weeks needed for the plants to grow. Most of the information for this simple exercise will be given on the back of the seed packet.

To make the maximum use of the available soil, some vegetables, such as cabbages, cauliflowers and leeks, can be grown in a seedbed until they are large enough to transplant, and then they can be planted in their cropping area. This is a very helpful technique that can be introduced on a wide range of vegetables, and is invaluable for plants that would otherwise occupy the ground for a long period of time at a wide plant spacing. The disadvantage of transplanting young plants is that the disruption may check their growth unless they are kept well watered so that they establish and grow quickly. This is particularly critical where the transplants are dug up from a seedbed and replanted; some roots will always be damaged by this process, and a good supply of water is essential to help these plants recover. If they are short of water, many vegetables will "bolt" – that is, the plant will stop growing leaves and develop instead a flower-bearing stem in an attempt to produce seeds.

A timing guide to successional sowings is to make the next sowing when the previous sowing has germinated and emerged through the soil.

Crop rotation

When groups of related vegetables are grown on a different plot from year to year, this is called crop rotation. One reason for moving crops from one part of the plot to another is to avoid the build-up of diseases and pests in the soil. Another benefit is that the soil's fertility can be improved by growing crops that add nitrogen, such as peas and most beans. Start by making a list of the various vegetables you intend to grow, and then classify them into groups based on their needs in terms of space and growth patterns.

Allocate each rotation group to a plot of land, and draw up a month-by-month cropping timetable. This will keep the land fully occupied and provide continuity. For example, after Brussels sprouts and leeks are finished in early spring, follow with sowings of peas, carrots, lettuces or scallions.

If you prefer, the vegetables can be from different crop groupings, which means that the rotation from one plot to another is a gradual process, rather than a wholesale changeover on a certain date.

If there is not enough space in a small garden to rotate entire blocks of vegetable crops, you could grow the plants in narrow strips instead and then regularly swap the groups between the strips.

Grouping the different types of vegetables together makes crop management easier. Leave at least two years before planting any vegetable from the same group on the same ground.

Crop rotation groups

This plot is divided into three groups: peas and beans (left), brassicas and leafy crops (middle), and roots and stems (right). A fourth, permanent, plot can be created for crops that are not shifted, such as asparagus. Each group is moved each year onto a new strip of land.

Multi-row bed system

Where space is limited, a special, multi-row bed system can be introduced. This has more, narrower beds than a conventional plot, and several rows of plants are grown more closely together than usual. With this multi-row system, the beds are only 3–5ft (0.9–1.5m) wide and the center of the bed can be reached from a path, so there is no need to walk on the soil and possibly crush it when tending plants. For several rows the plants are grown close together, with the distance between the rows being the same as the distance between the plants.

With such close spacing more plants can be grown per square yard (square meter) than by using a conventional system, in which plants are usually grown 1–2ft (45–60cm) apart. In the multi-row system the pathways, at 2–2½ft (60–75cm) across, are slightly wider than those on the conventional system, which are generally about 1½ft (45cm) across.

By growing plants closer together, the competition for space between plants can be used to restrict the ultimate size of the individual vegetables. This can mean that having a small vegetable plot works as an advantage, and often the close spacing of plants reduces the amount of weeding necessary because the weeds are smothered.

However, such close planting does not work with all vegetables: lettuces, for example, will not form good hearts if they are grown at close spacings, unless a naturally small cultivar is chosen.

Making the best use of available space
Summer and winter cabbages are interspersed in rows. As one row is harvested before the other, there is room for the remainder to grow.

Intercropping

The space between crops that are slow growing or need a wide spacing can be used to grow quick-maturing crops such as radishes, lettuces, kohlrabi or turnip, which are harvested before the main crop is large enough to fill its allotted space. However, careful timing is important.

Such gaps between crops within a bed can also prove invaluable as seedbeds for other vegetables, which will later need to be transplanted into permanent positions at much wider spacings.

Maximum yields
Radishes and turnip make excellent catch crops when planted at the same time as later-maturing brassicas.

Extending the season

By making the most of your plot you can harvest crops year-round. This can be achieved by careful planning and successional sowings, growing several types of the same crop and protecting the plants from frost. If protection is used carefully and effectively, the growing season can be advanced throughout spring or run well into the fall and winter months.

For raising young plants, a cold frame with a glass or plastic top can be used to acclimatize them before they are planted out. Plastic sheeting and polytunnels warm the soil before planting and are invaluable for protecting young or overwintering plants. Floating mulches, such as fleece, laid over the crop or suspended on hoops, will also protect early crops.

Growing under glass

To establish early crops, a large number of vegetables, such as leeks and brassicas, can be sown in containers in a greenhouse. Other crops, like cucumbers and melons, need such a frost-free environment at all times.

Plants dislike very hot temperatures, so apply a shading paint to the glass in late spring and always ensure that the greenhouse is well ventilated during the day. Plants will require copious watering.

Using grow bags

Grow bags contain a peat-based compost with added nutrients sufficient to establish most plants. Plants grown in grow bags will need additional feeding throughout the year.

Traditionally grow bags were used to grow outdoor tomatoes and placed against a warm wall with canes to which the plants could be trained. However, the range of vegetables that can be cultivated in grow bags is actually much larger. Suitable vegetables include lettuces, peas, green beans, spinach or perpetual beet. Peas can be allowed to sprawl over the sides of the bag rather than being trained upwards on twigs. This also serves to hide the bags.

Forcing crops
Tuck in plastic sheeting with an edging knife over soil that needs warming before planting.

Hardening off young plants
Gradually open the cold frame lid to harden off young plants.

Gardening with grow bags is simplicity itself. Put the bag in position and make a number of holes in the base according to the instructions on the side. Cut out the squares on the top of the bag and insert the plants. A normal bag can cultivate three tomato plants, but if you plan to use one for lettuces or peas then these can be planted quite densely. Plants need to be fed regularly with liquid fertilizer. Aim to cover the whole surface of the grow bag when the plants are mature.

Grow bag problems

There are two main problems with grow bags. They need to be watered properly every day in summer: modern bags often incorporate a plastic funnel that conveys water along the length. They need also to be concealed for they are not things of any great beauty.

If you have an established patio kitchen garden then you can construct special boxes or troughs into which new bags can be placed each year or you can have a sunken space on the terrace the right dimensions to take a new bag. This is an excellent idea if you are planning to grow vegetables, such as peas or tomatoes in grow bags each year, for it lowers the bag to ground level making it less conspicuous and trailing plants will hide the plastic relatively quickly.

Watering grow bags
Tomatoes are perfect for growing next to a sunny wall in a grow bag. They will need watering often, especially in hot weather.

Growing under cover

Growing vegetables under cover, whether under glass or plastic, allows gardeners to extend both their repertoire of vegetables and the length of the season in which they can be grown. Yields are generally higher under cover and the quality better. Wind and storms need not be a worry and pests, such as rabbits, birds, cabbage root fly and carrot fly, can be easily excluded, while others, such as whitefly and red spider mite, can be more effectively controlled.

The ideal form of winter protection for vegetables is a greenhouse. However, many gardeners do not have room for such a large item. Fortunately, where space is a problem, low mini-polytunnels, cold frames and cloches can perform part of a greenhouse's functions. Albeit on a much smaller scale, they will still be able to heat up the soil and offer light and warmth, plus protection from extremes of weather and many pests.

Polytunnels

Plastic polytunnels provide many of the advantages of a greenhouse and are a fraction of the price. They can be erected in a couple of hours and then taken down and stored when not required – although they can be a bit of an eyesore.

However, if you have the space in your garden then polytunnels will enable you to produce crops a good six weeks ahead of those grown in the open, which means you will be able to raise two crops a year instead of one. Low polytunnels are particularly useful as protection for crops prone to flying pests, birds and carrot flies. These can be homemade with a length of tough polythene, galvanized wire hoops and some twine and posts.

In very cold weather, protect overwintering plants – such as fava beans – with a plastic tunnel.

Cold frames

The basic construction of a cold frame consists of a box with wooden or brick sides, covered over with a glass or plastic lid, often sloping. You can make a cold frame yourself quite easily by simply placing a sheet of plastic over a wooden box.

Cold frames are useful for hardening off greenhouse-grown plants and raising seedlings. They can also be used for growing tender plants, such as eggplant, peppers, melons and cucumbers, as well as protecting hardier crops.

To work to their full capacity, they should be put in a sheltered place where they get maximum exposure to the sun. On hot days, prop the lid open to prevent overheating, while during cold, frosty spells spread old carpet, sacking or newspaper over the top as insulation.

Cloches

Cloches are simple plastic or glass tents, which are smaller than cold frames and portable, and as such are used to protect plants that are grown out. A glass cloche will hold the heat better than plastic, and being heavier it is less prone to being blown away. Glass is also less likely to become brittle and crack, although it is generally more delicate to handle.

Cloches are useful for drying out and warming soil prior to planting, and will protect seedlings and hasten their growth. They will also harden off greenhouse-grown plants and, for older plants, they offer protection against pests, will speed up the ripening process and extend the growing season. They can even be used to protect some crops throughout winter.

Other forms of protection

Frost protection fleece and even a humble sheet of plastic will also help out the vegetable gardener by warming and drying out soil, thereby protecting plants from extremes of cold and also pests. Frost protection fleece operates differently from plastic, as it allows light, air and water to pass through it, enabling plants to breathe. It is also lighter than plastic. Given all these characteristics it can be left on top of the crops as they mature, keeping off many pests and preventing wind damage.

An outside cover for onions. If they are pulled in wet weather let them dry before storing over the winter.

In very hard weather, containers can be wrapped in bubble wrap, weighed down with a stone.

Watering

Plants, whether they have just germinated or are heavily mature, must have water for growth. Most plants have critical periods when water is especially vital, so the skill in providing an optimum water supply is to know when and how to apply the water.

The amount of water your plants require depends upon weather and soil conditions, as well as the health of the individual plant. Young plants and seedlings need frequent light watering. Try to ensure that they get a good soak every few days – once plants are mature, frequent light watering simply encourages their roots to stay near the surface rather than growing deep down into the ground.

Leafy salad crops will need extra water in dry periods to prevent them from running to seed, while the fruiting vegetables need more attention in terms of watering when their flowers appear and when the fruits and pods are growing.

Follow these basic rules:

- At the seed and seedling stage, to aid establishment. Water the seed drills with a fine watering can until they have developed a deep root system.
- After transplanting, to aid reestablishment. Leave a slight depression in the soil at the base of each stem, then fill it with water.
- To produce crops. Fruiting crops such as tomato and scarlet runner most need water while flowering and when the fruit starts to swell. Leafy crops need heavy watering about 15 days before harvesting. Root crops should have a steady supply of water from sowing through to cropping.

A gravel container filled with water enables the plant to draw up the moisture it needs in a gradual way without the compost becoming waterlogged. This is the watering principle adopted in many greenhouses.

If a plant appears totally dead and dried out it is worth plunging the pot and plant in a bucket of water and leaving it there until the bubbles have stopped rising to the surface. There is a chance that it may well recover.

The best times to water vegetables are early mornings or evenings when the sun is less intense, reducing the amount of moisture lost to evaporation.

Watering container plants

Watering is the most important part of vegetable container gardening and without water the plants will die. If you can install an automatic watering system, this will solve all problems.

There is absolutely no point in attempting to grow plants in containers, outside, in the summer, unless you are able to water them every day. That is not to say that they have to be watered every day. If it rains all week you certainly won't, but if you go away on vacation for two weeks and this coincides with a hot dry spell don't be surprised if half your vegetables are dead when you return.

Plants grown in containers need far more moisture than plants grown in the garden. A large container 36in (90cm) in diameter may lose up to 1.1 gallons (5 liters) of water each day through the leaves of the plants (transpiration) and evaporation from the container itself, when it is hot and sunny. Terracotta containers are more subject to evaporation than plastic ones, but you can overcome this if you line earthenware pots with plastic sheets when they are planted.

Watering systems

With a large vegetable garden it is well worth installing an automatic watering system. These are computer-controlled and if you have one then all worries about watering vanish. There are three main systems: overhead sprinklers, trickle tubes and capillary systems. All have their advantages and disadvantages. Overhead sprinklers are probably the cheapest to install but they use the most water. Trickle hoses are more expensive but more effective. They deliver water directly to the roots of the plants. Capillary systems are expensive but useful for large areas requiring frequent irrigation.

WATERING

Watering is essential especially in summer and needs to be done every day in hot dry weather. Fill the container to the brim and let the surplus water drain away. Do not just sprinkle the plant and container lightly with water. This will do more harm than good.

Be careful when you water any acid-loving plants growing in ericaceous compost if you live in a hardwater area, as the leaves can turn yellow if the acid level in the compost changes. Either add a small amount of flowers of sulfur to the water or collect rain water in a barrel outside and use that.

Feeding

Vegetables need additional feeding to produce good crops, particularly those that are grown in containers. Liquid fertilizer is the easiest type of feed to apply. Leafy, root and fruiting vegetables have different requirements.

Good soil preparation will go a long way towards ensuring your plants have enough nutrients. Plants growing in soil that has had a large amount of organic manure dug into it for several years should hopefully not need extra feeding. However, the process of building up soil fertility can take a while to establish and in the meantime you may find it necessary to apply organic or chemical fertilizers to aid crop growth.

Vegetables, more than ornamental plants, are greedy for nutrients from the soil; in their growing season they put on a great deal of growth and may need an extra boost of feed. Vegetables grown in containers are particularly susceptible to shortages because the area and soil volume in containers is limited and because they are watered more frequently so the soil may be leached. So container-grown vegetables need regular feeding to thrive and produce the best crops.

Check the feed necessary for each plant and take care to apply the correct fertilizer at each stage of the plant's growth. Growing plants need a nitrogen-based fertilizer but you should switch to a potash- (potassium) based fertilizer as the plants reach maturity.

Mix any liquid feeds carefully in a can or spray can that can be kept specially for the purpose. Always follow the maker's instructions on the packet or bottle and do not be tempted to increase the strength of the solution as this may do more harm than good.

Foliar feeds are most effective during the summer and should be applied to the leaves on the "little and often" principle. Plants can be sprayed every two weeks with benefit. It is better to apply any foliar feeds with a small spray can as this is much more economical.

When to feed

If the soil is well nourished it should not need much additional fertilizer but a slow release feed in the spring is helpful to the young plants. During the growing season it might be necessary to use a quick-acting fertilizer as a boost. The quickest-acting feeds come in liquid form.

Liquid feeds

Liquid feeds are particularly useful for vegetables as they give a quick, easily accessible burst of nutrients during the growing season. These feeds are either designed to be applied to the soil or, for a very direct route into the plant, some are meant to be sprayed directly onto the leaves; these are called foliar feeds. With both of these it is very important to make sure that the mix is correct; if it is too strong it can burn leaves and young plants.

Check the instructions to see how often the plants need feeding and do not be tempted to over-feed the plants.

Slow and controlled release feeds

Slow release feeds are great for feeding the soil which will then feed the plants. These come in granular or powdered form and can be used in spring.

Controlled release feeds are granules that are mixed into the soil or compost. They are usually used in containers and some will keep providing feed for months on end and so provide a "once a season" feed.

Basic chemistry

The three main nutrients required by plants are nitrogen (N), phosphorus (P) and potassium (K), and are often referred to by just those symbols, NPK. Nitrogen is essential for healthy leaf growth, phosphorus for the development of proper root systems and potassium promotes the production of flowers and fruit.

Plants also need a number of trace elements, the most important of which are manganese and magnesium. Nutrients are present in varying proportions in all fertilizers and foliar feeds and are marked on the label. A balanced fertilizer will contain them in equal proportions. A high potash (potassium) feed is excellent for tomatoes and fruit when the plants are mature and bearing fruit, but all tender vegetables, such as peppers, require high nitrogen feeds when they are growing to help establish healthy plants.

General requirements

Nearly all vegetable crops need to be fed generously unless the soil they are growing in has been improved with organic manure over several years. They require nitrogen-based feeds when growth starts in spring followed by potassium-based fertilizer as the plants reach maturity. Apply fertilizers in liquid form during the growing season – use a liquid fertilizer or foliar feed. Slow-release granules, however, are invaluable. Add them to the soil at the start of the growing season and one application will serve many plants throughout the year.

Mulching

A weed is any plant growing in a place where it is not wanted. Many weeds cause problems just because they are so tough and versatile that they can adapt to a wide range of growing conditions. For this reason they must always be dealt with before they get out of control. The most effective way to prevent them from appearing in the first place is to use a mulch.

Mulching for weed control

Mulching is the practice of covering the soil around plants with a layer of material to block out the light and help trap moisture. In today's gardens, where plastics are commonplace, inorganic black plastic sheeting is often chosen. Though not inviting to look at, it can be hidden beneath a thin layer of more attractive natural, organic mulch.

As a general rule, organic mulches provide the bonus of improving the fertility of the soil, but inorganic mulches are more effective because they form a better weed barrier. To be fully effective as a barrier, organic mulches must be applied as a layer at least 4in (10cm) thick. Both organic and inorganic mulches tend to be less effective against established perennial weeds, unless an entire area can be sealed until the weeds have died out and planting is carried out through the mulch while it is in place. One way of clearing weedy ground in summer is to cover the soil with a mulch of clear or white plastic, sealed around the edges. Weeds are gradually killed by a combination of high temperatures and lack of carbon dioxide.

The plastic sheeting can be removed after a time and used elsewhere. The treated area is weed-free, ready to plant and cover with an organic mulch, such as shredded bark or gravel (see below).

Gravel mulch
Covering the soil with a mulch such as gravel will block out light and prevent weed seeds from germinating.

Weeding

Weeds compete directly with your vegetables for light, nutrients and water. They can also act as hosts to pests and diseases (see pages 44–45), which can spread as the season progresses. Groundsel, for instance, often harbors the fungal diseases rust and mildew, and sap-sucking aphids. Chickweed also plays host to aphids as well as red spider mites.

Perennial weeds

Digging up perennial weeds is an effective disposal system, provided that every bit of the root system is removed from the soil. If only a few weeds are present, try digging them out with a knife or trowel, but you must remove the top 2in (5cm) of root close to the surface, to prevent the weed from re-growing. This is a reliable means of eradicating weeds growing close to garden plants. In this situation, often no other weed control method would be effective without risking damage to plants growing nearby.

Clearing weeds

The simplest way to deal with weeds is to remove them physically, either by pulling or digging them out or, if they are small, hoeing them off at soil level.

The biggest problem with this method of control is that most weed seeds require exposure to light before they germinate. Often, when weeding disturbs the soil, more air is allowed into the surface layers and an ideal seedbed is created. Although the existing weed seedlings are destroyed, the weed growth cycle starts all over again. This problem is often worse when using rotovators, because they leave the surface layers of soil light and fluffy, making a perfect seedbed. Perennial weeds are increased, too, because they are chopped into pieces, each capable of re-growing.

The most effective way to clear weeds, especially established perennials, is to use a combination of cultural and chemical methods. Spray weeds in full growth with a chemical herbicide and, as they start to die, bury them when the area is dug over. When the new weed seedlings germinate, spray them with a chemical while they are most vulnerable.

Annual weeds

Clearing annual weeds with a hoe is quick and effective, but the timing is important. The hoeing must be done when the weeds are tiny and before they start producing seed.

Hoeing will sever the stems of young weeds from the root system just below soil level. This both prevents the stem from forming new roots and stops the roots from producing a new stem. When hoeing, make sure you always walk backwards to avoid treading weeds back into the soil.

There is an old saying, "One year's seeds make seven years' weeds," which has now been endorsed by scientific research and proved to be remarkably accurate – unfortunately for gardeners.

Annual weeds are capable of producing a staggering total of 60,000 viable seeds per square yard, per year. The vast majority of these seeds are found in the uppermost 2in (5cm) of soil, but they will usually germinate only when exposed to sufficient light levels. This is why mulching (see opposite page), which covers the soil and blocks out light, has become such a widely popular method of weed control. The added benefit of mulching is that there is also little chance of contaminating the soil with chemical residue.

General care

It is important to ensure that your crops are not damaged by pests and diseases (see pages 44–45). To do this you can use organic or chemical methods.

Organic methods

Reaching for a chemical is not the only solution to an outbreak of pests or disease; there are many other preventative measures that can be taken. The first step is to grow healthy, vigorous plants because these seem less susceptible to attack, especially when there is also good garden hygiene (clean and healthy plants and materials) and crop rotation is carried out (see pages 28–29).

Physical barriers can be put in place to deny pests access to the crop: for example, lay mats around the bases of brassicas to keep cabbage root fly at bay, or cover your crops with fine nets, the edges of which should be buried in the soil to deter flying pests.

Traps of shallow dishes containing cola or beer can also be laid to entice crawling pests into them so they can be easily disposed of. Finally, organic sprays based on natural substances, such as rotenone, pyrethrin, insecticidal soaps and sulfur, are useful and very effective controls against a variety of pests and diseases.

Chemical methods

These can be very effective in pest and disease control, as long as they are used strictly according to the instructions on the container and are applied thoroughly. Their main drawbacks are:

- Some chemicals may kill beneficial insects as well as harmful ones.
- Certain chemicals are very long-lasting.
- Chemicals may taint the produce with residue.

Physical barriers
Nets will keep pests such as pheasants and pigeons off the crops. This is especially important when the plants are young.

Organic sprays
Lettuce plants are treated with a solution of insecticidal soap to kill aphids.

Protective barriers
A layer of netting protects succulent young vegetable plants from marauding birds.

Baited traps
Fill a sunken dish with beer to catch slugs and snails. The sticks help any beetles to escape.

Wasp traps
Hanging from a plum tree, this jar full of sweet-smelling liquid attracts wasps.

Pests and diseases

These are the major pests, diseases and other problems that affect vegetables. However, do not be alarmed, as although there are numerous things to be concerned about, your plants are unlikely to be troubled by all of these. For proven environmental reasons, there is a strong emphasis in these pages on non-chemical methods of control of the pests and diseases discussed.

Aphids

These are among the most troublesome of insect pests, particularly greenfly and blackfly, and they attack a wide range of plants. Wash off aphids with plain or soapy water, or spray with insecticidal soap if necessary.

Blight

Blight affects potato and outdoor tomato, especially in wet seasons. It can be identified by the brown patches which appear on the leaves and lead to rot. Prevent it by growing disease-resistant varieties, and control by spraying in the very early stages.

Blossom end rot

Blossom end rot affects tomatoes in particular, especially those grown in pots or grow bags, as this problem is commonly caused by underwatering. The first sign is the appearance of black patches underneath the fruit, which then rot. It cannot be cured, only prevented by regular watering and feeding.

Caterpillars

The caterpillars of various moths and butterflies eat holes in the leaves of numerous vegetables. They are usually green, brown or gray and are generally hairy. Caterpillars are easily picked off and destroyed, or plants can be sprayed with an insecticide if necessary.

Clubroot

Cabbage, cauliflower, Brussels sprout, rutabaga and turnip are among the plants prone to this disease, which causes growths to appear on the roots, wilting and rot. Prevent by liming the soil and adhering to a strict rotation plan. As there is no cure, remove and burn all affected plants.

Cutworms

These caterpillars, the larvae of several different moths and greenish brown or grayish brown in color, live in the soil and feed on roots and stem bases of plants, causing young plants to wilt and die. Remove any found during soil cultivations.

Damping off

This disease affects seedlings indoors, causing them to suddenly collapse and die. Damping off can spread rapidly and should be prevented by using sterilized compost and clean containers.

Earwigs

These nite-feeding insects, easily recognized by their rear pincers, eat holes in vegetables' leaves, flowers and buds. Remove and destroy any pests. Spray plants with an insecticide if necessary.

Flea beetles

Flea beetles are tiny black insects which jump high into the air when disturbed, and will eat holes in the foliage of all types of brassicas. Prevent them becoming a problem by clearing away all plant debris, where they overwinter, and protecting with fleece. Early and late sowings are safe from attack. Dusting with derris powder is another solution.

Gray mold

This major fungal disease, also known as botrytis, can infect all top growth of plants – flowers, buds, leaves and stems – resulting in rotting. Cut off any affected parts of plants, back to healthy tissue.

Leaf spot

Many diseases show up as brown or black spots on the leaves of numerous vegetables. The spots vary in size and some are in the form of rings. The best control method is to pick off any leaves showing spots. Spray affected plants with a fungicide if necessary.

Mildew

The most common is powdery mildew, appearing as white powdery patches on the leaves of many plants. Remove affected leaves. Spray plants with a fungicide if necessary.

Red spider mite

There are several kinds of these microscopic spider-like creatures that feed by sucking the sap from the leaves of many plants, particularly under glass. This results in fine pale yellow mottling on the upper leaf surfaces. Spraying plants regularly with plain water will deter the mites. Or spray plants with insecticidal soap.

Root rot

Root rot primarily affects bean, pea, tomato, cucumber and container-grown vegetables. It is a fungus which causes roots to turn black and the plants to wilt and die. Prevent the disease by practicing crop rotation, using sterilized compost and watering with mains water. Pull up and burn any diseased plants, and dig up and remove the soil around their roots, which will harbor spores.

Scab

There are various forms of scab. Potato scab manifests itself by growths on the tubers and is more of a problem where the soil is light. Again, choose disease-resistant varieties and practise good husbandry by clearing away plant debris in the fall.

Slugs and snails

Slugs and snails eat the leaves of a wide range of plants and also damage soft young stems and even flowers. Control them by placing slug pellets around plants. Alternatively, remove them by hand.

Verticillium

Verticillium wilt is a fungal infection mainly affecting plants grown in the greenhouse and will kill them after a few seasons. At the first sign of the disease – brown markings on the stems and roots – remove and destroy all affected plants; at other stages of the disease, plant foliage wilts and leaves may turn yellow or brown.

Viruses

Viruses are types of diseases that infect a wide range of plants. The most common symptoms are stunted and distorted plants. There is no cure: pull up and burn affected plants.

Weevils

These beetles are easily recognized by their elongated "snout." Their larvae are the main problem. Their feeding causes wilting, and invariably death in severe attacks. Use biological control with a pathogenic nematode in late summer.

Wilting leaves

Apart from wilting caused by various pests and diseases, the most common cause is drought. Young plants may never recover, even if watering is carried out. Make sure the soil never dries out, ideally by mulching permanent plants and by watering as necessary.

Woodlice

These pests feed at night and hide in dark places during the day. Physical control is not practical, except to ensure that any plant debris is not left lying around, which will encourage their appearance.

Harvesting, storing and freezing

When to harvest vegetables and how to store them will depend on a number of factors, including the time of year and the type of vegetable. Most vegetables are harvested when fully mature, but a few such as spinach can be cropped repeatedly as a cut-and-come-again crop.

Leafy vegetables, such as Brussels sprout, are quite hardy and will survive outdoors in temperatures well below freezing point. Many root vegetables, however, have a high moisture content and are easily damaged in winter, even if left in the soil. Exceptions to this are carrot, parsnip and rutabaga, which are particularly hardy and can be allowed to overwinter in the ground until they are required for consumption.

The main causes of deterioration during storage are moisture loss from the plant tissue (with beet and carrot in particular drying out very quickly), or infection and rotting of damaged tissue caused by rough handling when the vegetables were being harvested. Onion and potato both tend to bruise particularly easily.

Some vegetables such as onion, chilli pepper, pea, bean and garlic will keep quite well if stored in a dry condition. If they are not to deteriorate, they must be allowed to dehydrate slowly in a cool, dry place. Once dry, store beans and peas in airtight containers. Garlic, chilli peppers and onions can be hung up in an airy place. Any storage area must be frost-free.

Many vegetables also freeze well. These should be blanched before being cooled rapidly and frozen in sealed, airtight boxes or bags.

Ripe vegetables and fruit wait for no one. Always harvest your crops when they are ready and if they cannot be eaten straight away, dry them or freeze them for use later.

It is unlikely that the harvest from a container kitchen garden will be large enough to cause any major storage problems. However, that said, there is every reason to do what you can to ensure that nothing is wasted and that you are able to make the most of your harvest and enjoy all the fruit, vegetables and herbs that you have grown when you want to eat them.

Drying and storing

If you have sufficient space then a number of vegetables, such as onion and potato, can be dried off and stored in a cool dry, dark place for several weeks. Carrot and beet can also be stored in boxes of sand.

Drying chilli peppers Bulbous vegetables and chilli peppers should be hung up in an airy, frost-free place to dry.

Harvesting parsnips Parsnips can be left to overwinter in the soil and dug up as required.

Always harvest young vegetables when they are fresh; many become overripe quickly. Freeze any surplus that you cannot use right away.

	Crop rotation group	Ease of growing	pH range	Suitable for freezing	Length of growing season	Yield (lb per sq yd)	Tolerates frost
Asparagus	3	M	6.0–7.5	✓	52	3.3	✓
Beet	3	M	6.5–7.5	✓	8	4.4	✓
Belgian endive	2	D	6.5–7.5	✕	12	0.9	✓
Broccoli	2	M	6.0–7.0	✓	8	4.4	✓
Brussels sprout	2	E	6.0–7.5	✓	8	3.3	✓
Cabbage	2	E	6.5–7.5	✓	10	8.8	✓
Calabrese	2	E	6.5–7.5	✓	8	4.4	✕
Cardoon	3	D	6.5–7.5	✓	52	3.3	✓
Carrots	3	M	6.0–7.5	✓	8–12	4.4	✓
Corn salad	2	E	6.5–7.5	✕	8	2.2	✓
Cauliflower	2	D	7.0– 7.5	✓	8–10	10.0	✓
Celeriac	3	M	6.5–7.5	✓	14	6.6	✓
Celery	3	D	6.5–7.5	✓	14	8.8	✓
Chilli pepper	3	M	5.5–6.5	✓	9	3.3	✕
Chinese cabbage	2	E	6.5–7.5	✓	8	3.3	✕
Corn	3	E	6.0–7.0	✓	10	1.1	✕
Cucumber	3	E	5.5–6.5	✕	8	6.6	✕
Eggplant	3	E	5.5–6.5	✓	9	11.0	✕
Endive	2	M	6.5–7.5	✕	12	3.3	✓
Fava beans	1	M	6.5–7.5	✓	20	8.8	✓
Florence fennel	3	D	6.0–7.5	✕	12	6.6	✓
Green bean	1	D	6.5–7.5	✕	8	4.4	✕
Garlic	3	M	6.5–7.5	✕	12	4.4	✓
Globe artichoke	3	D	6.5–7.5	✓	52	3.3	✓
Kale	2	E	6.5–7.5	✓	10	3.3	✓
Kohlrabi	2	M	6.5–7.0	✓	6	5.5	✓
Leek	3	M	6.5–7.5	✓	18–20	3.3	✓
Lettuce	2	E	6.5–7.5	✕	7	2.2	✕
Mizuna greens	2	E	6.5–7.5	✓	10	3.3	✕
Okra	1	E	6.5–7.0	✕	7	4.4	✕
Onion	3	M	6.5–7.5	✓	10–26	3.3	✕
Bok choy	2	E	6.5–7.5	✓	✕	3.3	✕

	Crop rotation group	Ease of growing	pH range	Suitable for freezing	Length of growing season	Yield (lb per sq yd)	Tolerates frost
Parsnip	3	M	6.5–7.5	✓	14	3.3	✓
Pea	1	E	6.0–7.0	✓	12	6.6	✕
Pepper	3	E	5.5–6.5	✓	9	3.3	✕
Potato	3	E	5.5–6.5	✓	14–22	6.6	✕
Pumpkin	3	E	5.5–6.5	✓	8	6.6	✕
Radish	3	E	6.0–7.0	✕	3	0.9	✓
Rhubarb	3	E	6.5–7.5	✓	8	4.5	✕
Rocket	2	E	6.5–7.5	✕	10	1.1	✓
Salsify	3	M	6.5–7.5	✕	20	3.3	✓
Black salsify	3	M	6.5–7.5	✕	24	4.4	✓
Scarlet runner	1	E	6.5–7.5	✓	10	8.8	✕
Shallot	3	M	6.5–7.5	✓	10–26	3.3	✕
Lima bean	1	E	6.5–7.0	✓	10	5.5	✕
Snow pea	1	E	6.0–7.0	✕	12	3.3	✕
Sorrel	2	E	6.5–7.5	✕	10	1.1	✓
Spinach	2	E	6.5–7.5	✓	6	3.3	✓
Squash	3	E	5.5–6.5	✕	8	4.4	✕
Jerusalem artichoke	3	E	6.5–7.5	✕	52	5.5	✓
Rutabaga	3	E	6.0–7.0	✓	10	4.4	✓
Sweet peppers	3	M	5.5–6.5	✓	9	3.3	✕
Swiss chard	2	E	6.5–7.5	✕	9	2.2	✓
Tomato	3	E	5.5–6.5	✓	10	5.5	✕
Turnip	3	E	6.0–7.0	✓	6–10	3.3	✕
Winged peas	1	M	6.0–7.0	✕	7	2.2	✕
Zucchini	3	E	5.5–6.5	✓	8	4.4	✕

Crop rotation group = 1 Pea and bean, 2 Leaves and flower heads, 3 Roots, stems, and fruiting vegetables

Ease of growing = D difficult, M moderate, E easy

pH Range = Preferred pH

Suitable for freezing = ✓ yes, ✕ no

Length of growing season from outside planting (in weeks)

Yield = pounds per square yard

Tolerates frost =✓ yes, ✕ no

DIRECTORY

Salad Vegetables

Cichorium endivia

Endive

There are two types of endive: curly leaved endive, a low-growing plant that looks a bit like curly headed lettuce, and the broad-leaved Batavian endive, which has broader leaves and makes a more substantial and upright plant. In the kitchen, endive can be used in salads – young, new leaves are best for this – or braised in butter. Traditionally endives are blanched (grown away from light) to make them taste sweeter. Broad-leaved varieties produce attractive white leaves when blanched, although a number of varieties are self-blanching.

Sowing

Sow seed thinly in furrows ½in (13mm) deep and 12in (30cm) apart, from mid-spring onwards.

Cultivation

When the seedlings are 1in (2.5cm) high, thin them to 12in (30cm) apart. Once the plants reach 10in (25cm) across, place an upturned plate on the center of each to "blanch" the heart. Water well in dry weather or the plants will bolt.

Harvesting

The plants will be ready to harvest about three weeks after blanching. Cut off the heads just above ground level.

H 8in (20cm)
S 10in (25cm)

United States Department of Agriculture (USDA) Hardiness Zone 4-8

Direct sunlight

Eruca sativa

Rocket

This tender-looking plant is actually quite hardy and will survive winter temperatures down to just above freezing. The leaves have a strong, tangy flavor which increases in strength when the plant matures or is kept too dry. Rocket can be eaten raw or cooked, and grown as individual plants or harvested regularly as a cut-and-come-again crop. It makes an excellent addition to other leafy vegetables in a mixed salad.

Sowing

Sow seed in succession at three-week intervals from mid-spring to early summer. Sow in broad furrows to create a band of plants about 12in (30cm) wide. If sown in such broad furrows, weeds will be unable to establish themselves owing to the density of the plants.

Cultivation

Keep the plants well watered to promote rapid growth.

Harvesting

Either remove individual leaves from the plants, or cut the seedlings down to about 1in (2.5cm) above ground level, and wait for them to re-sprout before cutting again.

H 8–39in (20cm–100cm)

USDA Zone N/A

Direct sunlight

Lactuca sativa

Lettuce

There are many forms of this annual vegetable, grown for its fresh leaves which are a mainstay of summer salads. For best results, grow several types, such as romaines, cabbage heads and loose-leaf lettuces. Loose-leaf types are less likely to run to seed, and are tolerant of most growing conditions. Leaf color can vary from pale green to reddish brown, and cultivars such as "Green Ice" and "Red Sails" are quite deep rooting, making them ideal for dry soils. Harvesting can begin about 12 weeks after planting.

Sowing

Sow seed thinly in furrows ½in (13mm) deep and 14in (35cm) apart. Sowing at regular intervals from early spring through mid-summer will provide a succession of lettuces from early summer through mid-fall.

Cultivation

When the seedlings have developed two "true" leaves, thin to 12in (30cm) apart. In dry weather, keep the plants well watered in the last two weeks before harvesting, when they make the most growth.

Harvesting

Loose-leaf lettuces should be harvested by pulling away the outer rows of leaves from one or two large plants on a regular basis. Cut off the entire heads of other types.

H 8–12in (20–30cm)

USDA Zone N/A

Direct sunlight

Lepidium sativum

Cress

Cress is a traditional sprouting crop which many people grow in containers on a windowsill, often on paper. Cress is best grown either in spring or fall, as it runs to seed quickly and does not relish hot weather; the plants should be kept well watered, especially in dry weather. Land, or American, cress is a good alternative to watercress and has a similar flavor. It may also be cooked. It makes a good filler for the container garden; a few seeds can be sown in situ either to grow in between other vegetables or as a border around the edge of the container.

Sowing

Sow a few seeds in situ throughout the summer. Seed sown in July and August will provide plants in the fall.

Cultivation

Thin plants to 6in (15cm) apart.

Harvesting

Plants are ready about eight weeks after sowing. Pick leaves as required.

H 2–5in (5–12cm)

USDA Zone N/A

Direct sunlight

Rumex acetosa

Sorrel

This versatile plant is an incredibly hardy perennial which is also very easy to grow. The tasty leaves have a sharp flavor and can be used fresh in salads or as a flavoring for soups.

Sorrel will grow on a range of soils, but prefers well-drained yet moisture-retentive, fertile conditions.

Sowing

In fall or spring, sow seed in furrows ½in (13mm) deep and 12–16in (30–40cm) apart.

Cultivation

Thin the seedlings to 10–12in (25–30cm) apart. Remove any flowers or seed heads as soon as they are spotted – this will preserve the plants' energy for leaf production – and replace the plants themselves every 4–5 years as their productivity declines.

Harvesting

Remove the outer leaves for use as they develop, and new leaves will continue to emerge from the center of the plant.

Valeriana locusta

Corn Salad

Also known as lamb's lettuce, this very hardy annual salad crop is grown for its mild-flavored leaves and will survive winter temperatures down to just above freezing. The erect-growing "French" cultivars are the hardiest; the "Dutch" and "English" forms have a much laxer growth habit, but are more productive. As it takes up very little room, corn salad is ideal for intercropping between slow-growing or tall vegetable crops. It will do well in most soils and is easy to grow.

Sowing

Sow seed in summer in furrows 6in (15cm) apart, with 1in (2.5cm) between the seeds. For year-round cropping, make an additional sowing in spring.

Cultivation

After germination, thin the seedlings to 4in (10cm) apart, and keep the seedbed well watered until they are about 1in (2.5cm) high.

Harvesting

Either remove individual leaves from the plants, or cut the whole head down to about 1in (2.5cm) above ground level to encourage fresh growth to be made, which can then be cut again for a further crop.

H 6–12in (15–30cm)

USDA Zone N/A

Partial shade

DIRECTORY

Fruiting Vegetables

Capsicum annuum Grossum Group

Sweet Pepper

These annual plants are grown for their characteristic bell-shaped fruits. When ripe, the fruits can be red, yellow, orange and even bluish-black, depending on which cultivars are grown. Sweet peppers prefer a deeply cultivated soil, but also do well in growing bags, pots and troughs; make sure the soil or potting mix is slightly acidic. They require an average temperature of around 70°F (21°C) and fairly high humidity.

Sowing

Sow seed singly in peat pots in mid-spring and germinate at 64°F (18°C). Young plants will be ready to plant out 10 weeks later.

Cultivation

Plant out 30in (75cm) apart. When the plants reach 30in (75cm) high, stake them individually and pinch back the growing point to encourage bushy growth. Spray them with water regularly to keep the humidity high. Once the fruits have started to develop, apply a high-potassium fertilizer every two weeks to encourage them to swell.

Harvesting

Pick the ripe peppers by cutting through the stalk about ¾in (2cm) from the top of the fruit.

H 24–36in (60–90cm)

USDA Zone N/A

Direct sunlight

Capsicum frutescens

Chilli Pepper

Also known as hot peppers, these plants are grown for their small, thin, tapering fruits which are green or red when mature, depending on the cultivars grown. The flavor is often very hot, with even the mildest increasing in strength as the fruits mature. The plants can grow up to 24in (60cm) high and 18in (45cm) across, while dwarf cultivars suit pots or growing bags. Chili and cayenne peppers require an average temperature of around 70°F (21°C) and fairly high humidity, so are often grown under protection.

Sowing

Sow seed singly in peat pots in mid-spring and germinate at 64°F (18°C).

Cultivation

Plant out 18in (45cm) apart, and when the plants reach 18in (45cm) high pinch back the growing point to encourage bushy growth. Spray the plants with water regularly to keep the humidity high.

Harvesting

When frost is imminent, pull up the plants and hang them upside down in a frost-free place, where they will continue to ripen and can be used as needed.

Lycopersicon esculentum

Tomato

Outdoor tomatoes are quite easy to grow and are among the best vegetables for the container gardener. They are attractive plants in both flower and fruit, and they do best in relatively warm climates, preferably in a sheltered position where they can be offered the protection of a south-facing wall. Tomatoes can be divided into two types, bush and cordon.

The cordon varieties are the most common and if they are to grow successfully they need to be trained up a cane or tied in to wires. Tie the plants in at regular intervals using garden string or raffia and pinch out all the side shoots where the leaf stalks join the stem. This leaves you with one straight stem and a number of trusses of fruit. When the fourth truss has developed small tomatoes, the growing tip should be pinched out, "stopped," two leaves above the truss. This allows the tomatoes to develop and ripen properly. If by any chance the summer ends rather earlier than it should and you are left with a large number of green tomatoes, these can be picked and brought inside and will ripen in the warmth of the house. Alternatively, you can use them to make green tomato chutney, a relish prized above many others.

Bush tomatoes are a bit simpler. These varieties grow either as small bushes, as the name implies, or trailing along the ground. They do not require either training or stopping but you do have to cover the ground to prevent

H 3–10ft (1–3m)

USDA Zone N/A

Direct sunlight

Lycopersicon esculentum (continued)

Tomato

dirt or damage to the fruit, a plastic sheet is the easiest thing to use on a patio, as many of the fruits are at ground level. Dwarf tomatoes, plants that grow little more than 8in (20cm) high, are very suitable for growing in window boxes and small pots but the yield is not large.

The flavor of tomatoes depends on the amount of sunshine they get and the amount of watering and feeding they have received, both of which can reduce the flavor. However, all tomatoes grown in containers or grow bags need plenty of watering and feeding as otherwise the yield will be minuscule.

Tomatoes prefer a fertile, well-cultivated soil. They will also grow successfully in pots, troughs and growing bags, but regular watering is essential to produce a good yield of large fruit. Cropping usually starts within 10 weeks of transplanting.

Sowing

For outdoor cultivation, sow seed in late spring. Place individual seeds in 4in (10cm) pots and germinate at 59°F (15°C), hardening the seedlings in a cold frame for 10 days before planting out.

Cultivation

The best growth is achieved at temperatures 68–78°F (20–25°C), and the plants and their fruits can be

Lycopersicon esculentum (continued)

Tomato

damaged when temperatures fall below 50°F (10°C), so in colder climates tomatoes are usually grown under glass or in plastic tunnels. Plant out the young plants as the first flowers open.

Plant out bush types first, because they are the hardiest group. Space the plants about 36in (90cm) apart: closer spacings will produce earlier crops, wider spacings a later but heavier yield. The plants can spread along the ground, perhaps on a mulch of straw or plastic. Plant cordon types at a spacing of 30in (75cm) and train them up stakes. Remove any side shoots as they develop, so the plant's energy goes into fruit production. As the fruits develop, apply a high-potassium fertilizer every two weeks to help them swell. When five fruit trusses have formed, remove the main stem at two leaves above this point, to encourage even growth. Then remove the stakes and lay the plants on straw to encourage quicker ripening. To extend the growing season, plastic tunnels can be used to protect the crops.

Harvesting

Pick the fruits as they ripen and remove any leaves covering the fruit to encourage more to do so. If frost threatens in fall, uproot the plants and hang up in a dry, frost-free place to allow the remaining fruits to ripen.

Solanum melongena

Eggplant

The eggplant is grown for its egg-shaped fruits, which are usually a blackish-purple but may be white-flushed or completely white in cultivars such as "Easter Egg." The plants can reach 30in (75cm) high and 2ft (60cm) across and have a deep root system. They therefore prefer a deep, fertile soil, but will also grow well in containers if fertilized and watered generously. Grow in a warm, sheltered spot.

Sowing

Sow seed in small pots in midspring, and germinate at 78°F (25°C). After germination, you will need to lower the temperature to about 62°F (16°C) – if higher than this, the plants will become spindly and prone to collapse.

Cultivation

Plant out as the first flowers start to open, but after there is little risk of frost. Space the plants 30in (75cm) apart, and stake them individually to provide extra support. When the main stem reaches 18in (45cm) high, pinch back the growing point to encourage bushy growth. Once the fruits have started to develop, apply a high-potassium fertilizer every two weeks to help them swell.

Harvesting

Pick the fruits when they are fully swollen, shiny, and firm with a smooth skin. If left too long before picking, the flesh will become bitter.

H 30in (75cm)
S 24in (60cm)

USDA Zone N/A

Direct sunlight

DIRECTORY

Squash Vegetables

Cucumis sativus

Cucumber

These tender plants are grown for their characteristic fruits with a high water content. Some cultivars have a bushy, compact habit while others can trail over several yards.

Cucumbers will not tolerate temperatures below 50°F (10°C), so a frost-free environment is essential. The plants will do well in soil-less potting mix in growing bags.The fruits will be ready to harvest about eight weeks after sowing.

Sowing

In mid-spring, sow seeds two to a 3in (7.5cm) pot in a temperature of 64–86°F (18–30°C). Thin to one seed per pot.

Cultivation

Once there is little risk of frost and the seedlings are 12in (30cm) high, gradually harden those to be grown outside. Plant at least 16–18in (40–45cm) apart, with 36in (90cm) between rows, to allow lots of light to reach the plants. Train trailing types vertically as cordons up nets or strings at least 6ft (2m) high. Twist support strings around the plants to hold them upright.

Harvesting

The fruits will be ready to harvest by late summer. Cut them from the plant, leaving a stalk of about 1in (2.5cm) on each fruit.

H 6–8ft (1.8–2.4m)

USDA Zone N/A

Direct sunlight

Cynara cardunculus Scolymus Group

Globe Artichoke

These large, bushy perennials are grown for their greenish-purple flower bracts and have a cropping life of three years.

Sowing

Sow seed 1in (2.5cm) deep in a seedbed in early spring in rows 12in (30cm) apart with 4in (10cm) between the seeds. Transplant into the cropping site in early summer. These seedlings will be variable, however, so division of named varieties is preferable.

Cultivation

Before planting, spread a 4in (10cm) layer of well-rotted manure and dig the ground to one spade's depth. Plant young side shoots 2in (5cm) deep and 36in (90cm) apart all around, and trim back the shoots by half their length to prevent wilting. After planting, spread a 4in (10cm) layer of manure around the plants to reduce weeds and moisture loss. Protect over winter with a layer of straw, until early spring, when each plant will produce two or three shoots to bear the flower heads.

Harvesting

From early summer to early fall, depending on the age of the plants, each stem will carry one primary flower head and several secondary ones. These should be cut when they are about 4in (10cm) across, removing each one with a 4in (10cm) section of stem.

Cucurbita pepo

Zucchini

Another member of the cucumber family, zucchini are a widely grown favorite summer vegetable. Those grown in the garden are far better to eat than any bought in a shop. The best zucchini to grow are the compact bush varieties; provided the fruits are harvested regularly, they will continue to produce fruit over a long period.

Grown for their long, cylindrical fruits, zucchini come in a range of colors from white, through gray, to deep green; some cultivars, such as "Spineless Beauty," are a mixture of green and cream-white stripes. The fruits, with their smooth, shiny skin, will be ready to harvest about 6–8 weeks after sowing.

Although any variety of these immature squashes can be eaten when young, it is best to choose a modern hybrid variety of zucchini. Numerous new cultivars have been introduced, with fruit colors ranging from the dark green of "Embassy," through lighter shades, to the yellow of "Gold Rush."

Sowing

In spring, soak the seeds overnite and then sow individually in 3in (7.5cm) peat pots at a temperature of 59°F (15°C).

H To 36in (90cm)
S To 36in (90cm)

USDA Zone N/A

Direct sunlight

Cucurbita pepo (continued)

Zucchini

Cultivation

Harden off the young plants before planting out. Plant bush types 36in (90cm) apart; trailing cultivars will need at least 6ft (2m) all around unless trained vertically, when they can be planted at the same spacing as bush types. Immediately after planting out, make sure that the plants are protected from overnite frost.

Each plant needs a minimum of 3 gallons (13.5 liters) of water per week. Mulch with a layer of organic matter at least 4in (10cm) deep, to retain soil moisture. Cut away any leaves shading the fruits. As the fruits start to swell, remove any male flowers close by to prevent the fruits developing a bitter taste.

Harvesting

Although they can grow much larger, zucchini are usually harvested when the fruits are 4–6in (10–15cm) long. Regular picking encourages the production of further flowers and fruits. Towards the end of the season allow one or two fruits to mature into giants. These can then be stored for several months in an airy, frost-free environment. Remember to avoid leaving them too long or they will become tough. Pick when the fruits are 10in (25cm) long – if your thumbnail goes in easily, they are ready.

Cucurbita maxima, C. moschata

Squashes and Pumpkins

Pumpkins belong to the same family as zucchini, and come in a wide range of shapes, sizes and colors. They are not suitable for a patio garden with limited room, but there is no doubt that a traditional orange pumpkin is a triumph for the gardener at Halloween.

These tender plants are grown for their unusual fruits, which vary tremendously in shape and size – from the large, orange fruits of the traditional Halloween pumpkin to the curved shape of crookneck and the distinctive "Turk's turban" squash. They can weigh up to 500lb (227kg) each and come in a range of colors from yellow to gray-green.

Squashes, crooknecks and pumpkins grow best in a warm, sheltered position and are generally ready to harvest seven weeks after sowing. "Gold Bar" is a useful cultivar, producing fruits weighing up to 2lb (1kg). "Park's" crookneck has fewer spines so is less prickly to harvest.

Sowing

In mid- to late spring, soak the seeds overnite in cold water and then sow individually in 3in (7.5cm) pots. Raise at 54–57°F (12–14°C).

Cultivation

Harden off the young plants for 2–3 weeks before planting out once there is little risk of frost. However, if frost is forecast, make sure that the plants are protected with

H 3–4ft (90cm–1.2m)

USDA Zone N/A

Partial shade

Cucurbita maxima, C. moschata (continued)

Squashes and Pumpkins

fleece. Plant bush types 36in (90cm) apart; trailing cultivars need at least 6ft (2m) all around.

Each plant requires a minimum of 3 gallons (13.5 liters) of water per week. Mulch with a layer of organic matter at least 4in (10cm) deep, to retain soil moisture. Cut away any leaves that shade the fruits. As the fruits start to swell, remove any male flowers that are close by to prevent the fruits developing a bitter taste.

Harvesting

Although they can grow much larger, the fruits are usually harvested when 8–10in (20–25cm) across, or when the foliage starts to turn yellow and the fruit stems start to crack. This is often just before the first hard frost occurs. After severing the fruit from the parent plant, dry it for about 10 days outdoors, using the warmth of the sun to improve storage quality. Then place the fruit in a string or netting bag, and hang it in an airy, frost-free place at a temperature of 50°F (10°C) for up to six months.

Protecting seedlings

Inverted jam jars can be used to protect young plants.

Ripening pumpkins

Lay black plastic sheeting underneath ripening pumpkins, crooknecks and other squashes to keep them off the ground.

Zea mays

Corn

Corn is the modern descendant of a very ancient plant native to Central America. Not surprisingly, it is more at home in a Mediterranean climate than in a cool temperate one, but given purpose-bred varieties and a good summer, there is every chance of success in reasonably mild regions. The site should be open and must receive plenty of sun. A soil well supplied with garden compost or manure and sufficient lime to correct strong acidity is also necessary. In order to get good results, corn must have a long growing season. Modern varieties will be ready for picking about four months after sowing. However, you must balance this with having the plants inside and protected while there is still a risk of spring frosts. Sow the seeds, therefore, in a greenhouse in mid-spring or in a cold frame from mid- to late spring. Plant the seedlings out when the risk of frost is over. If you do not have either a greenhouse or cold frame, you can sow the seeds where the plants are to grow outdoors in late spring or early summer. Once established, keep weeds at bay to avoid competition. When hoeing, be careful not to disturb, and certainly not damage, the surface roots; these are important feeding roots as well as the plant's main support. Provide plenty of water in dry weather. Do not plant traditional and

H To 8ft (2.5m)

USDA Zone N/A

Direct sunlight

Zea mays (continued)

Corn

supersweet varieties together, as cross-pollination can affect the quality of the supersweets.

Sowing

Sow seed under protection, with three seeds to a 3in (7.5cm) pot. Outdoors, sow seed from mid-spring in a seedbed in a warm, sheltered spot.

Cultivation

Corn relies on the wind to pollinate the plants. To facilitate this, plant in square or rectangular, 6-row blocks, with the plants spaced 14in (35cm) apart all around. Before transplanting pot-grown seedlings, cover the planting area with black plastic to warm the soil. When the seedlings are 6–8in (15–20cm) high, insert the young plants into the soil through the plastic and shelter them from wind for the first week after planting. Most of the plants will produce four or five cobs – to get large cobs, water the plants well as the cobs are developing.

Harvesting

The cobs will be ready to harvest from mid-summer to mid-fall. When the tassel ("silk") at the top of the cob starts to turn brown, snap the cob from the main stem.

DIRECTORY

Pod and Seed Vegetables

Abelmoschus esculentus

Okra

Grown for its elegant, edible pods, okra is nicknamed lady's finger because of its resemblance in shape. This tender vegetable must have as long a growing season as possible, because it will take at least seven weeks from sowing until harvesting the pods.

Sowing

In mid-spring, sow three seeds per 3in (7.5cm) pot at a temperature of 65–75°F (18–24°C). Thin the two smallest seedlings from each pot.

Cultivation

The plants should be 6–8in (15–20cm) high before they are planted out, usually from early summer onwards, once there is little risk of frost. Before planting, cover the planting area with black plastic for at least three weeks to warm the soil, and insert the young plants into the soil through the plastic. Space them at 14in (35cm) all around to encourage strong, bushy plants. They must be sheltered from winds for the first week after being planted.

Harvesting

From mid-summer until early fall, harvest the pods while they are still immature and before the seeds have developed fully. Cut them from the stem with a sharp knife. Harvest the pods as they form, to encourage the plant to produce more.

H 24–36in (60–90cm)

USDA Zone N/A

Direct sunlight

Pisum sativum

Pea

Garden peas are grown for their sweet-tasting, edible seeds, which are produced in green or (in a few cultivars) purple pods. The peas are generally round with a wrinkled or smooth skin, and can be eaten fresh – either cooked, or raw in salads – or dried and stored for use later.

The time from sowing to harvesting varies with each type. If you sow early crop peas in mid-spring, they will be ready to harvest 12 weeks later in mid-summer. Crops of maincrop cultivars will be ready to harvest about 10–12 weeks after sowing.

Sowing

Sow seed in flat-bottomed furrows 1–2in (2.5–5cm) deep. String foil across the rows to deter birds from taking the seeds or attacking the seedlings.

Cultivation

Keep the plants well watered from soon after flowering starts.

Harvesting

Start harvesting the pods when they are well developed but before they become too tightly packed with peas. Keep picking regularly to encourage further flowering.

H 18in–5ft (45cm–1.5m)

USDA Zone N/A

Partial shade

Pisum sativum var. *macrocarpon*

Snow Pea

Also known as mangetouts, snow peas are grown for their delicate, sweet-tasting pods, which are eaten young and whole. Alternatively, snow peas can be harvested later, in the same way as garden peas. They will be ready to harvest eight weeks after sowing.

Sowing

Sow seeds from mid-spring onwards at three-week intervals to provide a succession of crops throughout the summer. Sow in flat-bottomed furrows 1½in (4cm) wide and 6in (15cm) apart, with 4in (10cm) between the seeds. For cropping purposes, sow in blocks of three furrows, which can be separated from the next block by a 18in (45cm) path.

Cultivation

The crop is larger when the plants are supported by stakes, sticks, or plastic or wire mesh. With the three-row system, arrange the support over the rows in a tent-like structure, about 18–24in (45–60cm) tall.

Harvesting

The perfect stage for picking is when the peas are just visibly swelling in the pods. Harvest the pods by tugging them gently from the stem.

H 3–6ft (90cm–2m)

USDA Zone N/A

Partial shade

Phaseolus coccineus

Scarlet Runner

These easy-to-grow vines were originally introduced as ornamentals. Today, scarlet runner beans are grown mainly for their long, edible pods which are produced prolifically until the first frost.

Grown as annuals, scarlet runner beans require a sturdy support system, because they can reach heights of 8–10ft (2.5–3m) in their growing season of 10 weeks.

Sowing

Sow seeds in late spring or early summer – scarlet runner beans grow better in warm soil. Using a dibber, spot-sow 2in (5cm) deep in a double row spaced 2ft (60cm) apart and with 6in (15cm) between the seeds, to give the plants plenty of room as they grow. In colder areas, sow the beans indoors, two or three to a 6in (15cm) pot. Transplant when about 4in (10cm) tall.

Cultivation

Insert the supports when the plants are about 6in (15cm) high, just as the twining stem starts to develop in the tip of the plant. Water the roots well from soon after flowering and continue throughout the harvesting period.

Harvesting

The pods will be ready for picking from mid-summer onwards and harvesting can continue until the first frost, when the plants are killed.

H 8–10ft (2.5–3m)

USDA Zone N/A

Direct sunlight

Phaseolus lunatus

Lima Bean

Also known as the "butter bean," this plant is grown for its large, white seeds, although the young pods can be eaten whole about six weeks after sowing. The plants prefer a warm climate and a well-drained soil.

There are both bush and pole forms of the lima bean – the latter being useful in small gardens where space is at a premium. The beans will be ready to harvest 10 weeks after sowing.

Sowing

Sow seeds from late spring onwards 3in (7.5cm) deep and 12–18in (30–45cm) apart. Allow 30in (75cm) between the rows for pole cultivars, slightly less for bush forms.

Cultivation

Provide pole cultivars with stakes at least 6ft (1.8m) tall for adequate support. Once the plants reach 12in (30cm) high, supply a brand-name liquid fertilizer at two-week intervals to ensure growth, but stop fertilizing when the plants start to flower.

Harvesting

The beans will be ready to harvest when the swollen seeds are visible in the pods. Pull pods gently to prevent damage to the stems.

H 30in–6ft (75cm–1.8m)

USDA Zone N/A

Direct sunlight

Phaseolus vulgaris

Green Bean

Also known as French beans, green beans are grown for their curved, green pods which are eaten whole and for their partially developed seeds. Bush forms will grow 16–18in (40–45cm) high and 12–18in (30–45cm) wide. Pole cultivars can be grown up supports. Harvest eight weeks after sowing.

Sowing

Sow seeds at three-week intervals from late spring until mid-summer. Plant 2in (5cm) deep in double rows spaced 8in (20cm) apart, with about 6in (15cm) between seeds. Stagger them to give plenty of room.

Cultivation

Keep plants well watered once flowering starts to increase the crop and delay the onset of stringiness.

Harvesting

Pick regularly once the pods are about 4in (10cm) long and will snap cleanly in half.

Weather protection

A late crop of green beans should be protected by glass.

Psophocarpus tetragonolobus

Winged Pea

Winged peas are grown for their decorative, scarlet to chocolate-brown flowers, delicate bluish-green foliage, and triangular, "winged" pods that have an asparagus-like flavor. They are eaten whole. The pods will be ready for picking about eight weeks after sowing. However, do not expect large quantities of pods: even a heavy yield will be only about half that of garden peas. These plants grow best in a sunny position in a well-drained soil.

Sowing

Sow seed in mid- to late spring, in furrows about 1in (2.5cm) deep and 12in (30cm) apart, with about 12in (30cm) between the seeds.

Cultivation

Support the plants with stakes, sticks or plastic or wire mesh, or they will produce very few pods. Protection from birds is essential: suspending nets on stakes above the crop is the best method.

Harvesting

The pods are ready for picking from mid-summer until early fall. For the best flavor, harvest the pods while still immature and 1–2in (2.5–5cm) long. Pick regularly to encourage further flowering and the production of more pods.

H 18in (45cm)
S 24in (60cm)

USDA Zone N/A

Direct sunlight

Vicia faba

Fava Bean

Fava beans are very hardy plants, and will give a good crop with very little care and attention. They are grown mainly for their edible, greenish-white seeds, which develop inside thick, hairy pods, but the immature pods can be eaten when about 4in (10cm) long and the young shoots are also tasty. Those sown in fall will take up to 20 weeks to harvest; spring-sown crops are ready in 12 weeks.

Sowing

Seeds germinate better at lower temperature so sow in late fall (this will discourage aphids, to which fava beans are prone, since the plants will flower before the aphids are out in force) or in early spring. Using a dibber, spot-sow 2in (5cm) deep in a double row spaced at 12in (30cm) apart, with 10in (25cm) between the seeds to give plenty of room.

Cultivation

Most cultivars need support, and well-branched twigs 18in (45cm) tall will allow the plants to grow up through them. Water the plants well once flowering starts and throughout harvest-time.

Harvesting

If you sow in fall and spring, you should have fava beans for picking from late spring to mid-fall.

H 20in–6ft (50cm–1.8m)

USDA Zone N/A

Partial shade

DIRECTORY

Leafy Vegetables

Beta vulgaris Cicla Group

Swiss Chard

This hardy vegetable is grown for its large, glossy, succulent leaves, which can be up to 18in (45cm) long and 8in (20cm) wide. The brightly colored leaf stalks are red or white, and the leaves range in color from the deep green of "Fordhook Giant" to the lime-green of "Lucullus" or copper-green of "Rhubarb Chard." The best-known is red-stemmed Swiss chard, also known as ruby chard, which is easy to grow but prone to bolting, especially in hot, dry weather. Swiss chard prefers a fertile, well-drained but moisture-retentive soil.

Sowing

Incorporate plenty of organic matter into the soil before sowing. Sow seed for new plants at any time from early spring to mid-summer into furrows ¾in (2cm) deep and 18in (45cm) apart, with 6in (15cm) between the seeds.

Cultivation

When the seedlings are about 2in (5cm) high, thin them to 12in (30cm) apart – as a long-term crop, the plants need plenty of room or mildew may attack them. For cut-and-come-again crops, thin to 3in (7.5cm) apart.

Harvesting

Harvest the plants grown at wider spacings by cutting off the outer leaves at soil level.

Brassica oleracea Capitata Group

Cabbage

The tightly packed leaves and growing point of the cabbage plant are often referred to as the "head" or "heart," and this varies in size and shape – from round, through pointed to almost flat – according to type and cultivar. Growing a selection of the many types on offer makes it possible to have fresh cabbage available to eat year-round, harvesting even through quite severe winter conditions.

All types of cabbage are cultivated in much the same way, with the timing of sowing and planting varying according to the season, the cultivars chosen, and the time taken to reach maturity. The soil should be slightly alkaline to discourage a disease called club root, so apply lime if necessary.

Sowing

Sow seed thinly ¾in (2cm) deep in a well-prepared seedbed outdoors from mid- to late spring through to mid-summer, depending on the cabbage type. For many of the sowings, watering may be required to make sure the seedlings keep growing rapidly. If cabbages dry out, they will produce "hearts" too easily or "bolt" to produce seed.

Cultivation

Transplant the seedlings. Firm the soil well by treading it down before planting to encourage a strong root system which will support the plants. Plant out spring cabbages at a spacing of 12in (30cm) all around, summer and fall

H 12–18in (30–45cm)

USDA Zone N/A

Direct sunlight

Brassica oleracea Capitata Group (continued)

Cabbage

types at 16 x 18in (40 x 45cm) and hardy winter cabbages at a spacing of 20 x 20in (50 x 50cm) apart.

Harvesting

When the cabbage has developed a good-sized, solid heart, it is ready for harvesting. Using a sharp knife, cut through the main stem to remove the entire heart and a few outer leaves, leaving the oldest leaves and the stem in the soil.

How to transplant brassicas

When the seedlings have three or four "true" leaves, they are ready for transplanting into rows 12in (30cm) apart, with 18in (45cm) between the plants.

This crop matures quite rapidly and can take as little as 10 weeks from germination to harvest. However, because it is shallow rooted it is very important to keep the plants well watered.

1. Before transplanting, check that the growing point on a young plant is undamaged.
2. Embed the seedling to the depth of the lowest "true" leaves to stabilize the plants.
3. The plant is firmly enough planted only if a leaf snaps or tears when tugged.

Brassica oleracea Gemmifera Group

Brussels Sprout

These very hardy vegetables are grown for their edible flower buds, which form small, tight, "cabbage-like" sprouts in the leaf joints of the plant's main stem. Tall cultivars are ideal if space is limited, since they can be grown close together and produce a good "vertical" crop. The soil for Brussels sprouts should be slightly alkaline to discourage club root disease, so apply lime if necessary. They take about 12 weeks from sowing to harvesting.

Sowing

Sow seed thinly into a seedbed outdoors in mid- to late spring. Some watering may be required to make sure that the seedlings keep growing rapidly.

Cultivation

Firm the soil well by treading it down before planting to encourage a strong root system which will hold the plants erect. When the seedlings have developed three or four "true" leaves, transplant them into their cropping site with the rows 24in (60cm) apart and 24in (60cm) between the plants, firming each plant well into the soil.

Harvesting

The sprouts will be ready to harvest from early fall though to mid-spring, depending on the cultivar. To pick, pull the individual sprouts downwards so that they snap from the stem.

H 2–4ft (60cm–1.2m)

USDA Zone N/A

Direct sunlight

Brassica oleracea Acephala Group

Kale

This is the hardiest of annual winter vegetables. The soil for kale should be slightly alkaline to discourage club root, so apply lime if necessary.

Sowing

Sow seed in late spring outdoors in a seedbed. You may need to protect the seedlings against birds.

Cultivation

When the seedlings have developed four "true" leaves, transplant them into their cropping site, spacing the rows about 24in (60cm) apart, with 18in (45cm) between the plants. Water well until established.

Harvesting

Harvest on a cut-and-come-again basis from mid-fall to mid-spring by snapping off young leaves from all the plants. This will prevent any leaves from maturing and becoming tough and "stringy."

Hoeing between rows

Hoeing between kale plants controls weeds as they emerge.

H 12–24in (30–60cm)

USDA Zone 5-9

Partial shade

Brassica rapa Chinensis Group

Chinese Cabbage

This annual plant is grown for its crisp, delicately flavored leaves with white mid-ribs which are used fresh in salads. It is relatively fast growing and may be ready to harvest as little as eight weeks from germination.

Chinese cabbage resents root disturbance and is usually raised in pots. Transplant seedlings when three "true" leaves are about 2in (5cm) high.

Sowing

Sow seed individually in plastic or peat pots 3in (7.5cm) square in mid-summer. They need temperatures of 68–78°F (20–25°C) to germinate, so raise in a cold frame or greenhouse.

Cultivation

When the seedlings have developed four "true" leaves, transplant outdoors into rows about 12in (30cm) apart, with 18in (45cm) between the plants. Chinese cabbage is shallow rooted, and the plants must be kept well watered.

Harvesting

Starting in late summer, harvesting can last for up to 14 weeks with successional sowings. Cut through the stem just above ground level to remove the heart. The remaining stalk will often sprout clusters of new leaves, which can be harvested later on.

H 12–18in (30–45cm)

USDA Zone N/A

Direct sunlight

Brassica oleracea Italica Group

Purple Sprouting Broccoli

Grown for its edible flower heads, which are harvested while in tight bud, purple sprouting broccoli is a very hardy, biennial, winter vegetable. There are both white- and purple-flowered forms. The soil for broccoli should be slightly alkaline in order to discourage club root, so apply lime if necessary.

Sowing

Sow seeds individually in 2in (5cm) square plastic or peat pots, in a cold frame or unheated greenhouse in spring.

Cultivation

Plant out in early summer with 24in (60cm) between the plants all around. Water is essential to produce a good crop, the critical time being the first month after sowing. Surround young stems with extra soil to reduce wind rock.

Harvesting

Broccoli can be harvested from late winter until late spring and has a natural cut-and-come-again habit. Cut the central spike first, before the flowers start to open; side shoots will also try to flower and these smaller spikes can be cut later.

H To 24in (60cm)
S To 12in (30cm)

USDA Zone N/A

Direct sunlight

Brassica oleracea Botrytis Group

Cauliflower

Cauliflowers are grown for their edible flower heads, which are harvested while they are in tight bud. Cauliflowers can be available for most of the year, and certainly from early spring through to mid-winter. Fall- and spring-heading cauliflowers are the easiest to grow, often producing curds (immature flower heads) up to 12in (30cm) across. They will be ready to harvest in 8–10 weeks.

Cauliflowers are often judged on the whiteness and lack of blemishes on their curds. There are also forms with green and purple heads, which have an outstanding flavor.

Cauliflowers are among the most difficult vegetables to grow well. They need plenty of water to ensure rapid growth and resent root disturbance, so should be transplanted as young as possible, certainly within six weeks of germination. If transplanted too late or allowed to dry out at this stage, they may produce small, premature, tight curds which are tough and woody.

The soil for cauliflowers should be slightly alkaline to discourage club root and because acidic soils can promote some nutrient deficiencies, resulting in poor curds. (Apply lime if necessary.)

Sowing

Sow seeds individually in plastic or peat pots 3in (7.5cm) square, and raise in a cold frame or unheated greenhouse. Sow early summer cauliflowers in mid-fall for harvesting the

H To 24in (60cm)
S To 24in (60cm)

USDA Zone N/A

Direct sunlight

Brassica oleracea Botrytis Group (continued)

Cauliflower

following spring; fall cauliflowers in late spring for harvesting in fall; winter cauliflowers in late spring for harvesting the following winter; and sow spring cauliflowers in late spring for harvesting in early spring the following year.

Cultivation

When the seedlings have developed four "true" leaves, they are ready for transplanting to their cropping site. Spacing depends on the time of year; generally, the later the planting, the larger the cauliflower will grow and the greater the space needed for each plant. Early-summer cauliflowers, for example, should be planted at a spacing of 24 x 18in (60 x 45cm), winter cauliflowers at 30in (75cm) all around.

Harvesting

When the covering leaves start to open and show the enclosed curd beneath, the cauliflower is ready to harvest. Using a sharp knife, cut through the main stem to remove the complete curd, together with a row of leaves around it to protect the curd from damage and marking.

Brassica oleracea Italica Group

Broccoli/Calabrese

Grown as an annual for its edible flower heads, broccoli (also called calabrese) is similar to sprouting broccoli but less hardy, although it can be harvested in early spring if grown under protection. Many cultivars will mature within eight weeks of sowing.

Well-grown broccoli is tasty eaten fresh and ideal for freezing, the drawback being that the plant is very susceptible to mealy aphids, attracted to the flower spikes.

The soil for broccoli should be slightly alkaline in order to discourage club root, so apply lime if necessary. Broccoli resents root disturbance and often responds to transplanting by prematurely producing small, tight heads which can be tough and woody.

Sowing

Sow seed thinly in furrows 1in (2.5cm) deep and about 12in (30cm) apart, sowing three seeds ½in (13mm) apart in spots at 8in (20cm) intervals. Alternatively, sow seeds individually into 2in (5cm) diameter plastic or peat pots in a cold frame or unheated greenhouse if cold weather demands an earlier start.

Cultivation

When the seedlings have developed three "true" leaves, thin them to leave only the strongest and healthiest seedling at each spot. Transplant pot-grown seedlings at this point. Watering is essential to keep the plants growing

H To 24in (60cm)
S To 12in (30cm)

USDA Zone N/A

Direct sunlight

Brassica oleracea Italica Group (continued)

Broccoli

rapidly and to produce a good crop – critical times are the first month after sowing and the three-week period just before cropping commences.

Harvesting

The main cropping season is from early summer to mid-fall, but harvesting can continue until the plants are damaged by the first frost, before the flowers (usually yellow) start to open. The slightly smaller spikes produced by the side shoots can be cut later. Main-season plantings will often yield up to four or five cuttings before the plants are discarded. (They make useful compost.)

Applying lime

Lime can be applied at any time of year to raise the soil's pH but must be added alone, at least two to three months after manuring, or one month after fertilizing the soil. This is because lime and nitrogen react to release ammonia, which can harm plants.

If lime is used first, however, fertilizers and manures can be added just one month later. It is also simpler to add lime before crops are sown or transplanted into the site. If lime is applied too often, plants may show signs of nutrient deficiency. Bear in mind that it is easier to raise the soil pH than it is to lower it.

Brassica rapa var. *nipposinica*

Mizuna Greens

Grow Mizuna greens as a cut-and-come-again crop. This plant will benefit from some protection from the sun in high summer.

Sowing

Sow thinly in drills from mid-summer, thinning out to about 6in (15cm) apart. Sow under cover in fall for a winter crop.

Cultivation

Keep weed-free, and well-watered. Use a net to protect Mizuna greens from pests.

Harvesting

Ready in three weeks. Pick the leaves as needed, leaving the plant in the ground to re-sprout.

Brassica rapa var. *chinensis*

Bok Choy

Closely related to the Chinese cabbage, all parts of the Bok choy plant can be eaten. Varieties differ in height from 3–4in (8–10cm) to 18in (45cm). Look for bolt-resistant varieties.

Sowing

Sow seeds in situ ½in (13mm) deep, in rows 12in (30cm) apart, every few weeks for a continuous crop. Thin according to the size desired: small, 6in (15cm) apart; medium 7in (18cm) apart; large 14in (35cm) apart. Sow under cover in fall for a winter crop.

Cultivation

Keep weed-free, and water well.

Harvesting

Ready in three weeks. Pick the leaves as needed, leaving the plant in the ground to re-sprout.

Spinacia oleracea

Spinach

This reasonably hardy vegetable is renowned for its strongly flavored, dark green leaves, which are rich in iron and vitamins.

Spinach prefers a well-drained but moisture-retentive, fertile soil which is high in nitrogen. It will tolerate light shade. Although a perennial, it is best grown as an annual in order to produce the most vigorous leaves. The plants will often "bolt" (run to seed) and develop seed in the first year, especially during periods of hot, dry weather.

Spinach is usually ready for eating about six weeks after sowing. Individual leaves can be removed, or the whole plant cut back to produce new leaves for cut-and-come-again harvesting.

Sowing

For a continuous supply, sow seed thinly in furrows at three-week intervals from early spring to mid-summer.

Cultivation

When the seedlings are 1in (2.5cm) high, thin them to 6in (15cm) apart. For cut-and-come-again crops, thin to 2in (5cm).

Harvesting

Harvest plants grown at wide spacings by cutting off the outer leaves at ground level.

H 12in (30cm)
S 12in (30cm)

USDA Zone 6-9

Direct sunlight

DIRECTORY

Stem Vegetables

Allium porrum

Leek

Like onions, you can sow leeks either in a heated greenhouse in mid- to late winter or outside in the early to mid-spring. In either event, plant the seedlings outside in their final position when they are about as thick as pencils.

To grow leeks plant out the seedlings in early to mid-summer. Make holes 6in (15cm) deep and 6in (15cm) apart and, having trimmed the roots back to about ½in (13mm) long, drop a plant into each hole. No firming in is needed, you merely pour water into the hole. This covers the roots with soil and ensures that the little plants will flourish.

One of the hardiest of winter vegetables, leeks have a long cropping season, from early fall, through winter, and into late spring of the following year.

Sowing

In late spring sow seed thinly, 1in (2.5cm) apart, in drills 1in (2.5cm) deep and 12in (30cm) apart.

Cultivation

Transplant seedlings when they are 8in (20cm) high, the main planting season being mid-summer. Incorporate a dressing of high-nitrogen fertilizer into the soil surface before planting.

Harvesting

Harvest leeks when their leaves start to hang down, from early fall onwards, by lifting them with a garden fork.

H 24in (60cm)
S 8in (20cm)

USDA Zone N/A

Direct sunlight

Apium graveolens

Celery

Celery is grown for its crisp, blanched leaf stalks, which can be white, pink or red. Newer, self-blanching forms are easier to grow since they do not need to be artificially blanched. Celery needs a sunny, open site with deep, stone-free, well-drained, fertile soil that has had plenty of organic matter incorporated. To prevent plants from "bolting" or producing stringy leaf stalks, keep them growing steadily.

Sowing

Sow seed in trays or peat pots under protection from early to late spring. Place seed on the surface of the potting mix. Self-blanching celery needs warmth to germinate – the temperature should be above 50°F (10°C).

Cultivation

About eight weeks after sowing, harden the seedlings in a cold frame. From late spring on, when the plants have developed five to six "true" leaves, plant them out. Celery needs plenty of water to grow quickly and remain crisp.

Harvesting

Harvesting for trench celery can begin in late fall, when the leaf stalks are crunchy to eat; the pink and red forms are the hardiest and will be harvested last. Dig out the soil around each plant, lift the celery, then cut off the head and roots. Self-blanching celery can be harvested from mid-summer onwards. Celery can be left in the ground over winter.

H 24in (60cm)
S 6in (15cm)

USDA Zone N/A

Direct sunlight

Apium graveolens Rapaceum Group

Celeriac

This vegetable is grown for its celery-flavored, swollen stem, which takes six months to mature after sowing. It can be cooked or used raw.

Grow celeriac in a sunny, open site in free-draining soil. It may eventually reach 30in (75cm) high.

Sowing

Sow seed in trays or modules under protection, at a temperature of 61°F (16°C) from early spring onwards for a continuous supply.

Cultivation

About six weeks after sowing, harden off the seedlings in a cold frame. Plant them out in rows 12in (30cm) apart, with 16in (40cm) between the plants, with the stems just visible on the soil surface. In late fall, remove the outer leaves to encourage the stems to swell, and mulch with straw to protect from severe frost.

Harvesting

Harvest celeriac from late summer until the following spring, digging up the plants with a garden fork. However, plants will survive in the ground in most sites.

H 24in (60cm)
S 6in (15cm)

USDA Zone N/A

Direct sunlight

Asparagus officinalis

Asparagus

This herbaceous perennial can produce crops of its delicious shoots ("spears") for up to 25 years, so requires a permanent site.

Asparagus prefers deep, fertile, well-drained soil which has had plenty of organic matter incorporated into it 2–3 months before planting. In spring, before the spears emerge, the soil is often top-dressed with salt, which controls weeds but does not harm the crop.

Cultivation

Asparagus plants grown from seed give a variable crop, so it is best to purchase one-year-old asparagus crowns. Plant crowns in early spring, 4–6in (10–15cm) deep and 18in (45cm) apart, in ridge-bottomed trenches 12in (30cm) apart. Cut down and remove all top-growth in late fall as it turns yellow.

Harvesting

After the asparagus bed has been established for 1–2 years, you can then harvest the spears. Harvesting usually begins in mid-spring and lasts for eight weeks. When the spears are 6in (15cm) high, cut them with a sharp knife, slicing through the stem 1–1½in (2–3cm) below soil level. Keep the cut spears covered to prevent them drying out.

H 5ft (1.5m)
S 36in (90cm)

USDA Zone 4-9

Direct sunlight

Cynara cardunculus

Cardoon

Once its blanched stems were a popular vegetable, but now the cardoon is more often grown as a border plant for its dramatic foliage and thistle-like flowers. It grows to 6ft (1.8m).

Sowing

In late spring, sow three seeds per module under glass, thin to the strongest and plant out once all danger of frosts has passed. Or, station-sow in situ in early summer: sow three seeds 2in (5cm) deep in each station, leaving 24in (60cm) between stations. Thin out to the strongest.

Cultivation

Keep weed-free and well-watered in dry conditions. Feed weekly with a liquid fertilizer. Stake when the plant has grown to about 12in (30cm) high. Blanch in late summer or early fall: pull the stems loosely together and tie collars of newspaper or brown paper around the stems. Earth up the base and leave for four weeks.

Harvesting

Ready in six months. Dig up the plant and cut away the leaves and roots. Divide the roots, snip off the offsets and plant up for next year.

H 6ft (1.8m)
S 36in (90cm)

USDA Zone 7-9

Direct sunlight

Brassica oleracea Gongylodes Group

Kohlrabi

Kohlrabi is grown for its nutritious, globelike, swollen stem. There are green- and purple-skinned forms, both of which grow to 24in (60cm). Kohlrabi thrives in hot, dry conditions, and at the height of summer the stems will be ready to harvest eight weeks from sowing.

Sowing

Sow seed thinly in drills ¾in (2cm) deep and 12in (30cm) apart, in a well-prepared, finely sifted seedbed. Sow the quicker-maturing, green-skinned types from mid-spring to mid-summer, and the hardier, purple-skinned types from mid- to late summer.

Cultivation

When the first "true" leaf develops, thin seedlings to 8in (20cm) apart.

Harvesting

The swollen stems are ready when they are 3–4in (7.5–10cm) across. The newer cultivars can grow much larger, because they remain tender. Cut through the taproot just below the swollen stem.

Foeniculum vulgare Azoricum Group

Florence Fennel

Florence fennel is grown for its succulent bulb, which has a distinctive aniseed flavor, the edible part being the swollen bases of its decorative, feathery leaves.

It prefers well-drained but moisture-retentive, fertile soil which has had plenty of organic matter incorporated 6–8 weeks before planting. The bulbs are ready to harvest about 14 weeks after sowing.

Sowing

Sow seed in modules under protection from early spring onwards. Set in a temperature of 61°F (16°C) if growing in a greenhouse; seeds germinated in a polytunnel require 54–57°F (12–14°C), or 50°F (10°C) in a cold frame.

Cultivation

About six weeks after sowing, harden off the seedlings in a cold frame. Plant them out from early summer onwards, after two "true" leaves have developed, in rows 12in (30cm) apart and with 16in (40cm) between plants. When the bulbs begin to swell, cover the lower half with soil to blanch them.

Harvesting

The bulbs will be ready to harvest from late summer onwards, when they are 4in (10cm) across. Cut them off at soil level and trim away the leaves. Fennel can withstand light frost only, and does not store well.

H 24in (60m)
S 36in (90cm)

USDA Zone 4-9

Direct sunlight

Rheum x hybridum, syn. *R. x cultorum*

Rhubarb

Often regarded as a fruit, but technically a vegetable, this herbaceous perennial is grown for its edible leaf stalks, which can be used for desserts and jam-making from mid-spring onwards. Rhubarb, which matures to a height of 12in (30cm), can be grown in the same plot for many years, but the well-drained, fertile soil must be dug deeply and plenty of organic matter incorporated prior to planting.

Planting

In late fall, early winter, or spring plant one-year-old crowns about 3ft (1m) apart, with the young shoots ("eyes") just above soil level. If they are planted too deeply, the eyes will rot away.

Cultivation

Mulch the crowns well, keep the soil moist, and provide generous amounts of a balanced fertilizer after harvesting. Cut off any flowering spikes as they emerge in the spring and summer, and remove any spindly, unwanted leaves as they occur.

Harvesting

Pick the rhubarb when the stalks are 12in (30cm), long and deep pink in color. Grip each stalk as close to its base as possible and twist it gently away from the crown. Discard the leaves because they are toxic.

H 12in (30cm)
S 36in (90cm)

USDA Zone 7-9

Partial shade

directory

Bulb and Root Vegetables

Allium cepa

Onion

The strong-flavored bulbs of onions are invaluable in the kitchen for a wide range of dishes. They are grown as annual plants, with the brown- or yellow-skinned cultivars being the most popular with gardeners.

Onions have a long growing season, and for good skin quality and color the bulbs need plenty of bright sunshine in the period just before harvesting. Onions prefer a well-drained, fertile soil which has been well dug.

Sowing

In early fall or early spring, sow seed in furrows 1.5cm (½in) deep and about 12in (30cm) apart, with 1in (2.5cm) between the seeds.

Cultivation

Onions suffer from weed competition, and keeping the plants weed-free by hoeing between rows until they establish (this takes about six weeks) is critical.

Harvesting

Onions are ready for harvesting when the leaves turn yellow and the tops keel over. The process can be sped up by bending over the tops by hand, but this must be done carefully or the bulb may be bruised and will start to rot when in store. Lift the bulbs gently with a garden fork and allow them to dry naturally before storing in a cool, dry, frost-free place.

H 24in (60cm)
S 8in (20cm)

USDA Zone N/A

Direct sunlight

Allium cepa

Scallion

Also known as bunching onions or spring onions, they are fast-growing and can be used as an intercrop between larger-growing varieties or between carrots as a companion plant.

Sowing

Sow in drills every three to four weeks from early spring to late summer. Space seeds about 1¼in (3cm) apart with 6in (15cm) between rows. There is no need to thin further.

Cultivation

Keep weed-free, and water in dry conditions.

Harvesting

Ready in 8–10 weeks. As soon as they reach a reasonable size, pull alternate plants as needed.

Allium sativum

Garlic

This hardy vegetable, with its characteristic strong flavor that makes such a valuable contribution to both cooked dishes and salads, is far easier to grow than many gardeners realize. There are two distinct forms – one white and the other purple.

Garlic has a long growing period, but will survive outdoors in many areas throughout the winter if grown in a light, dry, well-drained soil. On wetter soils, the plants should be grown on ridges to improve drainage.

Sowing

Dig over the soil deeply before planting in fall. Split the bulbs into individual "cloves" and push these into the soil, so that the top (pointed end) of the clove is approximately 1in (2.5cm) below the soil surface. For maximum yields and even bulb development, plant the cloves in a square arrangement at a spacing of 7in (18cm).

Cultivation

As they develop, the bulbs will gradually work their way up to the surface of the soil.

Harvesting

The bulbs will be ready to harvest as soon as the leaves begin to turn from green to yellow. Lift the bulbs gently with a garden fork and allow them to dry naturally before storing in a cool, dry, frost-free place.

H 24in (60cm)
S 8in (20cm)

USDA Zone 3-8

Direct sunlight

Allium cepa Aggregatum Group

Shallot

Shallots have a very distinctive flavor and are easy to grow, but need a longer time in the ground than onions.

Sowing

Sow seed indoors in early spring, then plant outside in late spring, 6in (15cm) apart with 9–12in (23–30cm) between rows. Plant sets in situ in late winter (traditionally the shortest day), with the tips just showing, 6in (15cm) apart with 9–12in (23–30cm) between rows.

Cultivation

It is important to keep the site weed-free. Mulch to retain moisture. Water and feed spring-sown onions until mid-summer, then water only if they start to wilt. Feed overwintered bulbs once in early spring, cover with fleece to protect from frost if bulbs start to lift from the soil.

Harvesting

Ready in 26 weeks. Lift when the leaves die down, leave to dry out, then store as for onions. Healthy bulbs can be saved for replanting the following season.

H 24in (60cm)
S 8in (20cm)

USDA Zone N/A

Direct sunlight

Beta vulgaris

Beet

This useful root vegetable is a biennial plant which is grown as an annual and can be used at just about any time of year either fresh, stored, or pickled. Although the round beet is the most common, other shapes such as oval, flat, and oblong are also grown. There is also a wide variation in color – red being the most popular, but golden forms such as "Burpee's Golden" and white ones are available.

Sowing

Sow from mid-spring through late summer. Soak the seed in warm water for half an hour before sowing to promote rapid germination, then sow thinly in furrows ¾in (2cm) deep and 12in (30cm) apart.

Cultivation

When the seedlings are about 1in (2.5cm) high, thin them to 3–4in (7.5–10cm) apart for large beets, and 1½–2in (4–5cm) to produce small, round beets for pickling.

Harvesting

Harvesting usually runs from early summer to mid-fall, although beet can be harvested at any stage of growth depending on the size of beet required. The plants are not fully hardy, however, and should all be lifted for storage by late fall. Dig up the beet with a garden fork and twist off the leaves, then use immediately or store the roots in a box of moist sand in a cool, dry, frost-free place.

H 9in (23cm)
S 10in (25cm)

USDA Zone N/A

Partial shade

Brassica napus Napobrassica Group

Rutabaga

This cream- to purple-skinned vegetable is one of the hardiest of all root crops and is grown for its mild, sweet-tasting, yellow flesh. Good cultivars are "York" and "American Purple Tops."

Rutabaga, also known as swedes, require similar soil conditions to turnip. The roots will be ready to harvest about 24 weeks after sowing.

Sowing

Sow seed thinly in furrows ¾in (2cm) deep and 16in (40cm) apart in a finely sifted, well-prepared seedbed, from late spring onwards.

Cultivation

The soil should not be allowed to dry out at any stage, or a large proportion of the crop will develop forked roots and the plants may bolt. When the seedlings are 1in (2.5cm) high, thin them to 3–4in (7.5–10cm) apart, and then thin again three weeks later to leave the plants 10in (25cm) apart.

Harvesting

Rutabaga are usually ready to harvest from early to mid-fall onwards. Although they survive well outdoors through the winter, the low temperatures often give the flesh a fibrous or woody texture. It is therefore advisable to lift them and store indoors.

H 9in (23cm)
S 10in (25cm)

USDA Zone N/A

Partial shade

Brassica rapa Rapifera Group

Turnip

Often regarded as winter vegetables, turnip can be available throughout the year if a range of cultivars are grown in succession.

Turnip mature quickly and can easily be grown in a small container. They are mainly known as an ingredient of winter stews, but young turnip harvested when the size of golf balls are delicious.

Turnip prefer a light, fertile, well-drained but moisture-retentive soil which is high in nitrogen.

Sowing

Sow seed thinly in furrows ¾in (2cm) deep and 10–12in (25–30cm) apart in a finely sifted, well-prepared seedbed and subsequently at three-week intervals from late spring until mid- to late summer.

Cultivation

The soil should never be allowed to dry out, or much of the crop will develop forked roots and the plants may bolt. When seedlings are no higher than 1in (2.5cm), thin to 4in (10cm) apart for early cultivars, 6in (15cm) for later, hardy cultivars.

Harvesting

Turnip will be ready to harvest from early to mid-fall, but must be lifted by mid-winter.

H 12–24in (30–60cm)

USDA Zone N/A

Partial shade

Daucus carota

Carrot

Carrots are one of the most versatile of vegetables. You can grow them in one form or another throughout the year, from the young pencil carrots that are ready in early summer to the semi-mature roots that can be lifted later in the summer and through the fall. These are followed by the mature vegetables that are stored for use over the winter. Carrots must have a deep and fertile soil that is able to hold plenty of moisture. In particular, you need to grow the early varieties quickly if they are to be tender and tasty. Never grow carrots on land that has just had compost or manure dug in, as they usually produce divided roots. For the earliest crops of tender, young carrots, broadcast the seed, rather than sow it in rows, during early spring.

Cultivation

Thin the seedlings to 1½–2¾in (4–7cm) apart for medium-sized carrots, 2¾–4in (7–10cm) for larger carrots suitable for storing through the winter. Thinning is best done in the evening or in cool, dull conditions to deter carrot rust fly. Hoe between the rows until foliage shades the soil and reduces weeds.

Harvesting

Early carrots can be eased out with a fork and then pulled by hand. Dig up maincrop carrots with a fork for immediate use, freezing or storing. Twist off and then discard the foliage.

H 12in (30cm)
S 3in (8cm)

USDA Zone N/A

Direct sunlight

Helianthus tuberosus

Jerusalem Artichoke

Grown for its edible root, the hardy Jerusalem artichoke is also used to help clear rough ground. A vigorous perennial and relative of the sunflower, it can grow to a height of 10ft (3m), although the cultivar "Dwarf Sunray" will reach only about 6ft (2m).

Sowing

Plant purchased tubers in spring, 4–6in (10–15cm) deep, in deeply cultivated soil. Plant in rows 24in (60cm) apart, with 12in (30cm) between the tubers. Large tubers can be divided up so that each piece has a separate shoot, and the sections planted individually.

Cultivation

When the plants are 12in (30cm) high, mound up the soil 6in (15cm) high around the base to keep the plants stable. In summer, cut the stems down to 5ft (1.5m) to encourage tuber formation. In dry weather, irrigate to keep the tubers swelling.

Harvesting

The tubers are ready from mid-fall onwards and should be dug up with a garden fork. In well-drained soils, the tubers can be overwintered in the growing site. When harvesting, remove all parts of the tubers from the soil, or they will re-sprout next season.

H 6–10ft (2–3m)

USDA Zone 4-9

Direct sunlight

Pastinaca sativa

Parsnip

These winter vegetables have a very distinctive flavor and are hardy enough to overwinter in the soil. Parsnips prefer a deep, stone-free, well-drained, fertile soil, but on shallow soils shorter-rooted cultivars can be used.

Sowing

Sow seed thinly in furrows ½in (13mm) deep and 12in (30cm) apart, in early spring. Fresh seed gives the best results.

Cultivation

When the seedlings are about 1in (2.5cm) high, thin them to 2¾–4in (7–10cm) apart to produce large roots suitable for overwintering.

Harvesting

The roots will be ready to be lifted from mid-fall onwards. Dig them up with a fork.

H 12in (30cm)
S 3in (8cm)

USDA Zone 3-11

Partial shade

Raphanus sativus

Radish

One of the easiest of all vegetables to grow, radishes are the best way to introduce children to gardening. They germinate easily and mature quickly, in about a month. Gardeners with large vegetable gardens often use them as a marker crop between rows of vegetables that take longer to germinate and for the adventurous there are a number of winter-maturing radishes and the giant Japanese mooli radishes.

Sowing

Sow seed thinly in furrows ½in (13mm) deep and about 6in (15cm) apart. For a continuous supply, sow seed at 10-day intervals from early spring through early fall. The seed will keep for up to10 years if kept cool and stored in an airtight container.

Cultivation

Radishes produce poor plants if overcrowded, and ideally they should be about 1in (2.5cm) apart. Watering is essential: drought will make the roots woody or encourage the plants to bolt.

Harvesting

Radishes are ready to harvest when the roots are about 1in (2.5cm) across at their widest point. Grip the plant firmly by its leaves and pull gently. If the soil is dry, water the plants the day before harvesting so that they will pull out of the ground easily.

H 12in (30cm)
S 3in (8cm)

USDA Zone N/A

Partial shade

Scorzonera hispanica

Black Salsify

This hardy, perennial plant is, like carrots, usually grown as an annual for its thick, fleshy roots. These are about 8in (20cm) long and have a shiny, black skin – and a distinctive flavor when cooked. The young shoots (chards) and flower buds are also edible. It needs to have a deep, fertile soil in order to do well and produce a good crop.

Sowing

Sow seed thinly in furrows ½in (13mm) deep and 8in (20cm) apart, in spring.

Cultivation

Thin the seedlings to 4in (10cm) apart soon after germination. In order to achieve maximum growth, keep the plants weed-free and make sure they are well watered.

Harvesting

The roots will be ready to harvest from late fall onwards. In mild areas, the roots can be lifted and used immediately, but in colder areas they should be lifted and stored in boxes of sand before winter weather sets in.

Roots that are over-wintered in the ground can be covered with straw in early spring. Young shoots will emerge through the straw, and these (and the flower buds) can be harvested when they are about 4in (10cm) high.

H 24in (60cm)
S 12in (30cm)

USDA Zone N/A

Direct sunlight

Solanum tuberosum

Potato

This versatile vegetable is divided into three main groups: earlies (quicker-growing cultivars); main crop (slower-growing cultivars, producing heavier crops); and mid-season, which mature between the other two. Most early season potatoes are ready to harvest from early summer onwards, and do not store well. Main crop potatoes are available from mid-summer through into winter and can be stored.

Sowing

"Seed" is the term used for young potato tubers which are planted to produce the next crop. Purchase good-quality "seed" potatoes in late winter and arrange the tubers in shallow trays to chit in early spring.

Cultivation

In most areas, planting can commence from mid-spring onwards for earlies, finishing with the last of the maincrop tubers by early to mid-summer. Plant the tubers 16in (40cm) apart, in rows 2ft (60cm) apart.

Harvesting

Early potatoes are ready for lifting when the flowers start to open. To harvest, use a garden fork to dig under the ridge of earth and ease the tubers from the soil to avoid "stabbing" them.

Tragopogon porrifolius

Salsify

A hardy biennial plant, salsify is usually grown for its cream-white, fleshy roots, although its shoots are also edible. Because of its delicious flavor, it is often called the "vegetable oyster."

In order to achieve maximum growth, salsify requires a deep, well-drained fertile soil.

Sowing

Sow seed in furrows ½in (13mm) deep and 6in (15cm) apart, in spring. Fresh seed gives the best results, since salsify seed loses viability very quickly.

Cultivation

Thin the seedlings to 4in (10cm) apart soon after germination. To encourage rapid growth, keep the plants weed-free and well watered.

Harvesting

The roots will be ready to harvest from late fall onwards. In mild areas, the roots can be lifted and used as required, but in colder areas the roots should be lifted and stored in boxes of sand before winter frost sets in.

Glossary

Annual A plant that lives for one year only. Most vegetables are annuals.

Biennial A plant which lasts for two years. The first season is a leaf and shoot growing phase, during which energy is stored for the second season's flowering. Biennial vegetables are cropped after the first year. Examples include parsnips and carrots.

Bolting "Running to seed" or flowering before you want. In many cases this will ruin the vegetable you are trying to grow.

Catch cropping Sometimes one vegetable crop comes to an end a couple of months before you are ready to plant the next crop on that part of ground. Catch cropping is when you sow a quick maturing crop in this vacant gap.

Chitting Germinating seed before sowing. This is always done for potatoes, and may also be done for other seeds, such as corn, by placing them in a damp, warm place.

Green manure A crop grown specifically for digging back into the soil. These may be grown to protect the ground between crops, to stop nutrients leaking away, or to provide green matter and nitrogen ready for the next crops.

Half-hardy Plants unable to survive the winter without protection. Examples include scarlet runners and corn.

Harden off The gradual acclimatization of seedlings grown indoors or in greenhouses to outside conditions, before transplanting. This is often done in a cold frame which is gradually opened more and more each day to let in more "cold" air.

Hardy Plants able to survive the winter without protection. Examples of hardy vegetables include Brussels sprouts and broccoli.

Intercropping Growing small crops in the spaces alongside larger plants, or alongside plants which are so slow growing that before they reach maturity the smaller crop will have been harvested.

Mulch A layer of material placed over the ground, for the purposes of feeding the soil, conserving moisture, stopping weeds germinating, keeping the soil warm or protecting from heavy rain.

Offset A small, complete plant produced by many bulbous plants. It can be easily removed from the original bulb and planted on to produce another plant.

Perennial Plants that live for more than two years. Examples of vegetables that are left in the same spot for many years include rhubarb and asparagus.

Pricking out Moving tiny seedlings from pots or trays into new pots, to give them more room.

Seedbed A specific bed where seeds are sown for germination and development into small seedlings with the intention that they will later be transplanted to their final growing position.

Transplanting Taking seedlings from a seedbed or container and planting them where they will grow to maturity. Brassicas are usually transplanted (because they need more room when they grow to maturity than they do when just germinating). Root crops generally grow poorly after transplanting. In general, water the seedlings the day before you lift them, and water again after they have been planted in their new position.

True leaves When a seed germinates a pair of leaves is produced. The set of leaves to appear after these are the "true leaves." They look much more like smaller versions of the leaves of the mature plant.

Tuber The swollen part of a plant underground that stores energy. Potatoes are tubers.

Index